Keeping Up

Keeping Up

Blue Blazers,
Iced Tea, and Everything Else
Worthwhile in Life

JOHN BRIDGES

City Press Publishing, Inc.

Nashville, Tennessee

Library of Congress Cataloging-in-Publication Data
Bridges, John, 1950-
    Keeping up: blue blazers, iced tea, and everything else worthwhile in life/
John Bridges
    p. cm.
    Originally published in The Nashville scene as a column entitled
"Keeping up"
    ISBN 0-9638616-0-3: $11.95
    1. Southern States — Social life and customs — 1865- I. Title.
F216.2.B75   1993
975.04 — dc20   93-37424
                                                            CIP

Produced for City Press Publishing, Inc., by Zenda, Inc.
Cover and book design by Bruce Gore/Gore Studio, Inc.
Illustrations by Pat Patterson

City Press Publishing, Inc.
301 Broadway
Nashville, Tennessee 37201-2005

To Franklin,
who heard all these things first

CONTENTS

FOREWORD

by BRUCE DOBIE
Editor, *Nashville Scene*

The idea of a column called "Keeping Up" was hatched in the spring of 1989, over lunch at a Pargo's restaurant in Brentwood, Tennessee.

In retrospect, it was an ideal place for an editor and a writer to discuss a column about life in the modern South. Pargo's is a nuevo fern-bar chain from the fine folks who brought us Shoney's. The *Scene*, a newsweekly I had recently begun editing, was housed nearby in the Maryland Farms office park. The surrounding countryside was a web of glass and brick buildings, open meadows, sprawling strip mall-ettes, and condos. We were deep in the new, suburban, terra weirda. Nary a row of corn, or a cow, or any of the themes of the old, agrarian South could be seen.

I had never said more than ten words to John in my life, but I, like everyone in Nashville, knew him to be a great writer. In particular, I loved a story he wrote while he was still a music critic at *The Tennessean*. It was not a story about music. It was about seersucker suits. In one sense it was about pants, coats, and cloth, but it was mostly about history, etymology, culture, and everything that flowed from the idea of seersucker.

John arrived at lunch that day wearing a blue blazer with a big pocket handkerchief and two sets of glasses: regular old glasses on his nose, and pink reading glasses on his head. I thought Truman Capote had walked in.

"I think you could do something every week for the *Scene* much like you did on seersucker," I remember telling John. "Yes," he replied, "I could do martinis, for instance. But if you really want me to do this, I think I shall have to start with the picnic."

And so he wrote a column on picnicking in his old backyard with mama. In retrospect, I know John and I didn't really need to talk about his column at all. John already had the column within him. All it needed was a name and a page to run on. After the picnic column came the one on martinis. Then came pieces on dirt, white shirts, wedding dresses, and Chihuahua dogs. Stories came from his childhood in Slapout, Alabama. Stories came from time spent in nice bars having drinks with yuppie women in sun dresses. Stories came from Garth Brooks tunes, trips to the opera, the deaths of the stars.

The column works. It is consistently one of the most popular elements in the *Scene,* and no wonder. It has the charming sting of authenticity. Pat Conroy once observed that all Southern literature is a variation on one story: "On the night the hogs ate Willie, Mama died when she heard what Papa did with Sister." These days, this is a sad truth. Too much "Southern" writing follows a predictable plot line of old geezers, broken-down cars, small-town coots, and people who still can't get over the Civil War. John's stories, on the other hand, are about real people in today's South, the kind of folks who drive foreign cars, pay mortgages, have babies, drink too much — or don't drink at all.

Life in today's South sometimes seems a mad chase. Which is what John's column is all about. Some of his characters keep up. And some of them don't.

Keeping Up

In the Yard

This was not a picnic;
it was eating outside

 YEARS AGO, one late June evening in a front yard in Alabama, I signed an uneasy truce with summer.

Summer had an unfair advantage in the agreement. School had been out for all of three weeks, and already the air was itchy with kudzu. Nothing stirred.

The maid had taken to the back porch to do the ironing. From the darkness of a corner, a radio on a kitchen counter glowed dully and muttered nothing but farm reports and Connie Francis. Cotton was up. Connie sang "Where the Boys Are." Millet was down. Connie came back with "Who's Sorry Now?"

A tractor droned on in the field beyond the apple tree that flowered every year but never made any apples. Clouds of dust billowed up and settled sullenly down. There was no breeze. At noon, men came to the back door and ate food from used tinfoil pie plates. They drank iced water from quart canning jars left over from last year's pickled peaches. My mother snapped beans and talked on the phone.

Meanwhile, everybody I knew was at the lake. Just three weeks ago they had burst out of fifth grade, vowing to live until August in tree houses and pup tents only. They would play Roy

1

Rogers until sunset and stay up until ten. Time would be as nothing. They would agree to perform in a nonsinging version of *Rigoletto*. We would build the sets from old shirt cardboards, and I would be in charge.

Now they all had ear infections and impetigo. Everybody, the entire cast of *Rigoletto*, was smeared with purple medicine, and I would never be famous. My entire future was under siege. Summer—and being in Alabama and having to live with kudzu and crowder peas—had walled me in. There were no more opera broadcasts until December. Television offered nothing but "The Guiding Light" and "Lucy" reruns. I was trapped.

Weakly, I would wait for the bookmobile. I would check out *Quentin Durward* or *Quo Vadis* and make myself read it, dreary page after dreary page, while lying in bed in front of a window fan that roared and made the sad air whirl. The day-old bedsheets fluttered and snapped.

Summer, I figured, was something to survive. I had not yet learned about tans. I had never been to a beach.

Then, on this particular late June afternoon, with the window fan roaring, the bed linen flapping madly about in the sad spinning air, my mother appeared in the door. She smelled like snap beans.

"I've got an idea," she announced. "How would you like to eat outside tonight?"

In an instant, adventure came back into my life. What she was offering was not a picnic. It was Eating Outside. A picnic was pretty much an impossibility this far into a deepening Alabama summer. Heat and yellowjackets and chiggers—particularly chiggers—had long ago sapped every vestige of attractiveness from the exercise of eating stuffed eggs on a scratchy blanket infested with roly-poly bugs.

What my mother was offering was something different. It had nothing to do with paper plates and swatting away sweat bees. To Eat Outside was to insist that civilization was still possible, that courtliness and class distinctions still possessed a certain charm, that summer was indeed a season of leisureliness and languorous Southern nights. It had a great deal to do with having read too many books.

On this particular night ("I think it'll be cool enough," my mother had promised), there would be slices of tomato, onion, and cucumber soaked in vinegar and crusted with pepper. There would be potato salad on lettuce leaves, and there would be fried chicken, cooked that afternoon so that it was cold and nobody had to hurry to eat it.

There would be a guest, my Aunt Birdie Mae from across the road. She worked day-shift on the switchboard at a motel in Montgomery; her daughter had married well and moved to High Point.

Aunt Birdie Mae preferred to say that she lived "across the street." In her honor, my mother would open a can of asparagus. There would just be the three of us. My father had a sales meeting, and my brother was bagging groceries at the IGA until eight. My Uncle Jesse worked the night-shift at the Albert Pick.

My mother would spread a cloth printed with Mexican hat dancers over a rickety porch table meant for a fern, and we would use real plates and real knives and forks. We would drink iced tea from a pitcher; there would be sprigs of mint.

With a mimosa tree floating sickly sweet blossoms into the potato salad, we would dine while the twilight held its breath and Aunt Birdie Mae told tales of High Point. Cars would hum by on the highway; people would be amazed. When we were done, Aunt Birdie Mae scraped the dishes and helped my mother decide to dig up the mimosa. Then she went home. My father and my brother ate cold chicken at the kitchen table.

That very same night, long after we were supposed to be asleep, my father came to wake me and my brother. "You boys get up," he whispered—though there wasn't anybody else to waken—"Your mother has something she wants you to see."

We stumbled out to the side porch. My father had put on his pants, and my mother was wearing her housecoat. My Aunt

Birdie Mae and my Uncle Jesse had been called in from across the road. It had to be after midnight. The yellow bulb in the porch light made the air look orange. Beyond the porch screen the sky was black.

"You boys look," my mother said. "The night-blooming cereus has bloomed."

It was a single bloom, a lurid and licentious thing, hanging heavy and tropical from its stem. Its perfume made the whole night thick and slightly rank.

"It's beautiful, Sister," said my Aunt Birdie Mae. "Isn't it beautiful, boys?"

"You have to see this now," said my mother, "because it won't do it again tomorrow night."

"Why not?" asked my brother. "Because it just happens once," my mother said. "Now go back to bed."

"I think it smells," said my brother. "Go back to bed," my mother said. That night my parents left the porch door open, and the fan pulled the thick scent of the cereus through the house. "It smells," my brother said, fumbling and fretting with his sheets.

"Go back to sleep," said my mother through her bedroom door.

The next day, I forgot to check on the cereus bloom. A week later when I looked, it was wilted, dry, and brown. Back in my bedroom, however, I put on a performance of *Rigoletto* with my Walt Disney Television Theatre. Dopey had the title role; Alice in Wonderland played his daughter.

The Woman in Black

Before this night is over,
some guy is going to be history

A WOMAN IN A little black dress is a liar. Do not, under any circumstances, buy her dinner. She will not, I promise you, feel obligated.

The first problem is the dress itself. It claims to be little. And it is. It is very little. Its hem barely grazes the top of her knees. Its skirt rides snug and unforgiving around her hips. There are no sleeves. There are not even any straps. It consists mostly of bosom and leg. It consists, in fact, mostly of the woman in it.

She is a woman who considers this dress a wardrobe staple—a woman who honestly believes that this dress means to her upper thighs what a pair of Weejuns means to the feet of a lawyer in Paducah, Kentucky.

She is wrong. It took maybe two yards of fabric to make this dress, a dress that costs about $8,000. A cow died to make a pair of Weejuns. A pair of Weejuns goes for something like $89.95.

And you can wear a pair of Weejuns with jeans. On Saturday night. To buy some onion dip and a roll of TP at a Hot Stop market operated by people who still stick pictures of Ferdinand Marcos to the cash register with magnets shaped like A. J. Foyt. A woman can do a lot of things in a little black dress on a Saturday night. Very few of them, however, require a run for dip.

The dress, after all, is not only little. It is also Black. Coco Chanel came up with it because it reminded her of little Parisian shopgirls, who had only one dress and were, by necessity, Terribly Chic. A woman in a little black dress, however, is not working on commission. She does not know the aisle number for office supplies. She is never seen in places that even have aisle numbers. In places where she is seen, there are only floors. One is for silver. The other is not. She is never Mistaken for Help.

She fills grown men with a terror they have not known since a nun named Sister Fred made them stay after to dust the erasers in second grade. Sister Fred made them miss a game of stickball. This woman in the immobilizing black dress makes them miss the college graduation of boys young enough to be their sons. Women old enough to be their wives do not speak to them for weeks.

Mostly because of the dress. A woman with pale shoulders puts it on, and she thinks she is Catherine Deneuve in a two-page spread for perfume. She thinks she is a regretless Edith Piaf, baring her soul to a gray-skied, cobblestone-streeted world. She thinks she is Singer-Sargent's *Madame X,* her hair swept up, her bosom bare, and her face angled awkwardly away, poised in expectation of a slap. She thinks she is Holly Golightly and Anita Baker and anybody famous who ever wore a black dress, except maybe Julie Andrews trying to make it as a nun in *The Sound of Music.* Somehow, she has forgotten about Bloody Mary Tudor and the Wicked Witch of the West.

She puts on this dress, and, within minutes, she is leaning across a table, a final sip of sharp red wine rocking gently back and forth in the bottom of a glass that hangs heavy in her long, slim fingers. The light from a single candle, now little more than a stub of wick glowing dully in a pool of wax, turns her skin to porcelain. Her lips look very red. She runs a single long-nailed finger around the rim of the glass and lets the light from the candle glitter in her eyes.

The man with her is talking a great deal. He has already talked about his clients. And the series. And landfills. And His Son the Recent College Graduate.

Right now, he is talking about his option on a strip mall in Duluth, Minnesota. But he wants to be talking about her hair, the way it falls loose and shines against the useless light from the dying candle. He wants to be talking about the way she brushes it back to reveal the aching curve of her long, immaculate neck. He wants to be talking about the way it breaks free again and cascades down into one great golden wave.

He wants to be talking about the way she raises a hand and lets it linger over her own bare white shoulder, the way her palm brushes gently down her thin white arm, cold and glowing against the velvet blackness that is her dress. He wants to be talking about the way she quivers at her own touch, as if the touch of her own slim fingers against her pale, knowing flesh could warm her from the evening's chill. He wants to be talking about the way the candlelight glitters in her eyes as she looks up into his.

But mainly right now, he wants to be asking for the check. A waiter, a man desperate to be home watching "Columbo" reruns, has been pouring coffee at their table since 10:15. It is now 12:37 in the morning. The table is littered with little unused cups of creamer. There has been no Muzak since 11:45.

The man at the table scribbles his name on a credit card slip. He does not wait for a copy. He does not check to see that his carbons are torn. She asks for her coat. He is off to find it. Clattering against chairs and scraping the corners of tables, he fumbles back. He carries a gleaming black fur over one arm. He presses money into the waiter's outstretched palm.

Slowly she rises. The coat falls gently over her cool white shoulders. Its silken lining slides smoothly against the velvet blackness of her dress. His hands grip her trembling shoulders. She leans back heavily against his chest. She turns. A kiss grazes his cheek.

And then she is gone. Into a cab. A cab she has called for herself. While he was at the coat-check.

At the taxi door she pauses and raises a hand, not to wave but to warn him. "Lipstick," she says, mouthing the syllables soundlessly and brushing a single nail against her cheek before she disappears into the cab. Like clockwork, she pulls in a fold of black velvet and fur. It barely escapes the slamming door.

Domestic Engineering

Hot off the bus —
and looking for trouble

IT HAPPENED in one terrible moment — a horrid instant when I couldn't stand the sight of my bathtub, not for another minute. I called a cleaning service. I thought I would get a maid. I was wrong.

What I wanted was Ann B. Davis, a woman who could bring an end to unsightly grout without ever removing her cardigan sweater. I wanted Shirley Booth in a powder blue uniform with contrasting collar and cuffs. I knew she would be dizzy and prone to get too involved in my personal life. She would misunderstand phone messages and forget to tell me Ed McMahon had called to give me $10 million. But I would love her because she would bring order to my life and keep fresh Jell-O in the refrigerator at all times. She would simmer pots of stock and get the dust off the miniblinds. I would never have an unmatched sock again.

What I got, however, was a cleaning service. What I got was a person with a beeper and a business card with a picture of a dancing toiletbowl brush. A person with a minimum charge of $72.50 for three hours. A person with a File-o-Fax and an avocado-on-pita bread sandwich in a biodegradable plastic bag. I did not get Ann B. Davis. And I did not get a maid.

I know about maids. They are not people who get beeped.
They do not come from a cleaning service. They come from
somebody who knows your mother — either that or somebody
at the office, somebody who takes little mauve tablets in order
to remain calm.

Maids are not the type of people who leave a Post-It note on
the refrigerator door — a Post-It note with a cute little pink
kitty on it. The words coming out of the kitty's mouth say, "If
we're not Purr-fect, let us know."

The pink-kitty Post-It notes are left by People Who Clean,
people who think of you as a valued customer. Maids are
something else. They think of you as somebody with a television. They are not, after all, Ann B. Davis or Shirley Booth or
even Esther Rolle frying chick for Jessica Tandy with a look
that could kill.

Maids are Bette Davis in a rayon uniform poaching para-
keet for Joan Crawford's lunch tray. They are people who
come on a bus and enjoy control. Total control. If they do not
get it, they quit.

Maids do not request six-month performance evaluations.
If a maid leaves a note anywhere, it is written with a pencil —
a pencil you have not sharpened since you used it to flunk
make-up algebra in the summer of 1963. When a maid needs a
piece of paper, all she can find is the corner of a brown paper
grocery bag — a grocery bag that is precisely the same color as
the No. 2 lead pencils they used to make back in 1963.

Maids do not leave notes that ask you what you think. They
leave notes that say, "I need Soap." They underline Soap three
times.

Soap is important to them. If you do not buy them Soap,
they scorch your shirts. On the front. Right below the collar,
right next to the spot where your tie bursts out of its knot. It is
a spot everybody sees. All day long, people ask if there isn't
something brown on the front of your shirt.

Soap becomes very important to you as well. You stop on
the way home and buy it — in boxes and bottles and cans. You

buy soap that sprays, soap that foams, soap that turns Fresh Mint Green and works overnight to dissolve stubborn stains. You leave it on the kitchen counter. You draw a big red arrow on an index card. Above the arrow, in big red letters, you write, "SOAP."

At 6:45 that evening it is gone. The maid, however, has left another note. It says, "I need Pads—not Brillo." She only has to underline it once.

At 8:45 on a Sunday morning, when you are supposed to be playing squash on a court you've had reserved since sometime back in 1989, you go to the grocery store to buy Pads—not Brillo. They are not easy to find. You have to ask three stockboys and wait for a change of shifts between customer service representatives. It takes two and a half hours—to buy Pads.

You buy lots of them, a couple of cases. At home you put them on the counter, with another red arrow and an index-card sign that says, "Pads—not Brillo." You pray they are right. Otherwise, you know what will happen: She will put a blue ballpoint in the wash with your shorts. Then she will fold your shorts and leave them on the counter with a note. A note that says, "Sorry. Blue pen."

A cleaning service is concerned about keeping your business. They want you to Think of Them when you hear of others whose fine porcelain fixtures have been damaged by hard-water stains. They want you to know they will be gentle with your hand-washables and will never use harsh abrasives on tub or tile. They will dust and polish and scrub and shine. They have a motto. It says, "It is YOUR HOME, but you are OUR GUEST."

Maids, however, are not impressed. They have seen your blue underwear. They know you do not have cable in the den. They come into the kitchen while you are trying to eat a bran muffin and say things like, "Your commode's turning brown. Anybody around here gonna fix it?" They do not like the interior decorator. They hate the dog. The dog takes pills in order to remain calm.

You ask a maid, on Tuesday morning, to schedule chicken salad for three people, a week from next Thursday night, and she grows very quiet. She turns the iron up to "Linen" and puts it facedown on your shirt. She looks at you quietly and says, "We'll see."

It is the same look your mother gave you when you were in the third grade and asked if you could have a pony. You lived in a three-room apartment at the time.

You say, "Okay" and hope for the best. You do not feel good about this. You ask her, "When do you think I can know?"

She looks at you calmly and moves the iron a little to the left. "WE'LL SEE," she says. Her face has turned to stone.

"Okay," you say, your voice seeming oddly high and sweet as you attempt to back out of the room.

"I may need time off for this," she says, her voice drifting out from the washroom door.

"How much?" you ask.

"July," she says.

"That'll be fine," you say, doing a nervous little back-and-forth dance in the washroom door.

"I'll write it down," she says, taking a little red ring-type notebook out of her purse. She flips through its pages and scratches down a note. "I won't forget," she says, slipping the little red notebook back into her purse.

You look at her and smile, a nervous, angled smile. She smiles back. Her smile is big and calm and broad.

The click of her pen — it is a blue ballpoint; she lets you see it — cracks the air.

Fear Itself

A little speechless terror
never hurt anybody

I MUST HAVE been twenty-one before I ever had a truly convincing Halloween. Until I turned twenty-one, I spent most of my Halloweens in Alabama. In Alabama, when you're seven or eight or so and they don't carry candy corn at the Woolworth's, real, quality Halloweens are hard to find.

I knew what I wanted. I had seen *Meet Me in St. Louis*. I had seen Margaret O'Brien in a string of pearls and an old pair of high heels leading a troop of basically terrified seven-or-eight-year-olds with soot on their faces down a leaf-cluttered street lit by the helpless light of weak-eyed street lamps filtered through the creaking limbs of skeletal elm trees.

The wind groaned through the limbs of the bone-bare trees and made them scratch and scrape against one another. On every house an unlatched shutter banged. In every yard a mixed-breed dog barked madly with the primitive terror known only to a scruff-necked creature tortured by the shriek of cries beyond the catch of human hearing. At every corner a fleshless cat burst out screeching from under a clangoring pile of overturned garbage pails, a streak of pain shot screaming out of the blackness.

What had once been a street where children rolled hoops and icemen made deliveries was now a circle deep in the night of Dante's Inferno. Perfectly nice turn-of-the-century children—children who took piano lessons and sang "Under the Bamboo Tree" with Judy Garland—were transformed into languageless Angles and Jutes, their faces afire with the blaze of a bonfire built of apple crates provided by the corner grocer.

They were driven mad with the desire to bob for apples. To eat popcorn balls held together with a glue of simple syrup. To ring doorbells and run screaming into the night.

They would be home in time for supper at seven. But, for the moment, without ever having purchased an album by Motley Crüe or having ever watched a video involving Madonna and a group of lithe young men with inventive hair, they had become Beasts. Animals. They wanted to roll lawns. If they had known about toilet paper, they would have draped it from trees.

This is the Halloween I craved. I wanted to be scared skinless in the company of people I knew. I wanted to make myself so nervous that I might throw up at any minute. I wanted to be afraid. And then I wanted to go home.

Instead, I got a carnival staged by the PTA to raise funds for a mimeograph machine and an extra can of sweeping compound. I got fifty-eight kids in the same Casper the Friendly Ghost suit from the V.J. Elmore five-and-dime. I got a House of Horrors booth which consisted mainly of my mother's second cousin, Cora, wearing an afghan and attempting to convince seven-year-olds that a piece of liver was, in fact, a human brain.

I got to eat hot dogs. I got to play Go Fish and hook a brown paper sack containing two balloons, a whistle—which my father later hated—and a piece of Double Bubble—which later had to be removed from my hair with a piece of ice. I got to wear a penguin costume made by my mother from my own design. She had used two black buttons for the eyes and an old coat hanger to stiffen the beak. The feet were bright orange felt, and I couldn't use my hands because of the fins.

During the Costume Walk, I waddled twice around the stage and did not receive an Honorable Mention. The three top prizes—all of which were seventy-nine-cent boxes of chocolate-covered cherries—went to two Caspers and a Clarabell the Clown suit, which had apparently been purchased in Montgomery.

This was not the Halloween I had had in mind. I had not won anything all night long. And I had not been afraid. Not once.

Outside, no wind moaned through the bluish-black evening, here at the still-warm end of an Alabama October. No clawlike leaves rattled down to grapple their paper-dry fingernails into our hair. A distant dog barked. Somebody yelled at him, and he stopped.

Because it was a long way to walk, my parents drove me home. I sat in the back seat and flipped my penguin beak up so I could see the roadside fly past.

It was years later before I really learned to be afraid of anything—anything other than a *C* on a trig test or the chance that I might never learn to parallel park and would have to let my brother and his girlfriend drive me everywhere for the rest of my life. It was years later, when I was almost twenty-one, that I learned to be afraid. The year I turned twenty-one, they created the draft lottery, and my birthday came up Number 69. They drew the numbers one evening, but the next morning the numbers were still there. In the newspaper.

I tried getting sick. It didn't help. I hoped it would turn out that this was a joke somehow involving my mother's second cousin Cora in a Richard Nixon outfit. It wasn't.

The numbers didn't go away. Not for a long time. Neither did Nixon. Or "Three's Company." Or Jesse Helms. Or AIDS.

I missed having the Halloween I meant. I missed walking down a terrible street and finding out the next morning it was a place I knew. I missed clustering with friends around a bonfire hot with the blaze of apple crates from the corner store. I missed ringing the doorbell of a horrible neighbor and then dashing, frantic with laughter, into the night.

I'd like to try it now, I think. And then, if I could get a ride, I'd like to go home.

Swimming Upstream

Any place that serves raw fish
is no place for your mother

I WENT TO A sushi bar the other night. It was not a new experience. I go out for sushi a lot, whenever I have the desire to spend a lot of money and still feel like I forgot to eat.

This particular night I was meeting my friend the makeup artist and her friend the prop person, who was somebody I had met one time before. They were both in the music industry, and sushi is the sort of thing people in the music industry eat—mostly because raw fish comes out of the water, and water makes them think of the Coast.

Because everything on the menu has a strange name, music industry people in sushi bars can order smelt eggs and pretend they are speaking in code. They also like sushi because they feel it will make them small, which is important because they are all trying hard to think about what it would be like if they had hypnosis and really tried not to smoke.

My friend the makeup artist practically lives on yellowtail and avocado spring roll. She has her own private bottle of low-sodium soy sauce filed away for safekeeping behind the bar. She also thinks she used to know the sushi chef from when she lived in La Jolla, but she thinks maybe he spoke more English then.

The other night she told me, "We're going for sushi. If you get there first, do not take a table. We sit at the bar."

I did not get there first, mainly because I stopped at a cash machine for extra money. I thought this was the sort of night when maybe, just once, I would like to go to bed feeling like I had had something to eat.

My friend the makeup artist and her friend the prop person, whom I'm sure I had met once, were already at the bar drinking sake. They were also drinking Japanese beers. They had already ordered their sushi, but they said that good sushi can take a long time and that maybe I should have a beer too.

I said, "I think maybe I'm having a cocktail."

The prop person said, "That could be a very dumb move."

My friend the makeup artist said that nobody in a sushi bar ever orders cocktails. She said that the only things anybody drinks in a sushi bar are sake and beer. She said, if I ordered a martini, somebody would make it with Japanese gin. She said neither she nor anybody else had ever seen the person who mixes the cocktails in a sushi bar. She said she was sticking with beer. She said she was sticking with something that came in a bottle with a label she could read.

I said I did not want a beer. I told the cocktail waitress I would have something simple. I said I would have gin on the rocks with a splash of soda. I said that would not be hard to make. The cocktail waitress handed me a damp washcloth.

I said, "The only thing is, when I say soda, I don't mean Coca-Cola." I said this because I had had sushi lots and lots of times before. The cocktail waitress handed me a pair of chopsticks. She smiled a sweet unconfused smile and said, "Gin."

Behind the bar, the sushi chef was making a California roll. He was using lots of rice and a sheet of seaweed. He held up something that looked like a boutonniere made out of alfalfa and announced, "Japanese marijuana." All the Japanese-looking people at the sushi bar laughed. Then he stuffed the alfalfa sprouts into the California roll too.

The cocktail waitress stopped by to tell me she did not have any Coca-Cola. She said, "We only have Pepsi." I told her a beer would be fine.

The sushi chef handed me a crunchy shrimp roll and put a wind-up toy on top of the counter. It was a little pink plastic wind-up re-creation of a private part of the male anatomy. It looked, for the most part, precise in the important details, except that it could walk on its own. It had two little red chicken legs, and, when the sushi chef wound it up, it waddled down the counter between the yellow and red plastic mums. When it almost waddled into the sea urchin, the sushi chef caught it in his right hand, where it kept on trying to waddle with its little red chicken legs waving in the air.

All the Japanese-looking people at the sushi bar laughed. The sushi chef held up the little winding-down pink-plastic private thing and happily announced, "New Orleans."

My new friend the prop person was lighting a cigarette. She said maybe I should eat some fresh ginger. She said the fresh ginger would help me stay small.

Everybody at the sushi bar was either a music-industry-looking person or a person who had a really good chance of being Japanese—except for one gray-suited guy who came in with somebody who was probably his mother. They were waiting because they had ordered tempura. My friend the makeup artist stirred her chopstick around in a little green lump of wasabi and said, "My dears, get a load of this guy."

The gray-suited guy leaned over to my friend the prop person and pointed to the motherlike somebody on his left. He said, "When we came in here, she asked me what kind of place this was. I told her she could read the sign. I told her it said 'Sissy Bar.'"

I told my friend the prop person to tell the guy in the gray suit that everybody in the sushi bar was a drag queen except for him and me. My friend the prop person said she thought it was time for more ginger. My friend the makeup artist said she thought it was time for the check.

The sushi chef said we couldn't leave yet. He said we hadn't seen his latest trick. He said it was called "The Japanese Cucumber." He said the ladies liked it a lot. I told him to show it to the guy in the gray suit and his mother. I told him I had been to a sushi bar before. I told him I had seen the Japanese Cucumber too. I told him I was stopping by the grocery store on the way home. I told him I was buying bagels and cream cheese. I told him I would never be hungry again.

Pilgrimage

At Graceland, even off-season, some memories die hard

T HE FIRST TIME I went to Graceland, I went because it was work. A magazine out of New York wanted a story on the lingering fascination of Elvis Presley, the maybe-not-dead-yet King of Rock 'n' Roll, who maybe did — or maybe didn't — die in 1977 in an upstairs Graceland bathroom. My New York editor said I should go to The Source. He said I should take the Full Tour. He said, if it was at all possible, I should try to see The Commode. He said he would pay mileage. That is why I went.

I did not get to see The Commode. In the company of a minivan-load of people — most of whom were speaking Romanian, unless they were from Cleveland, Ohio — I got to see fourteen television sets and a room with shag carpet on the ceiling.

I got to see three display cases full of jumpsuits, some of which had capes. A tour guide named Kim explained that the Aztec jumpsuit was Elvis's personal favorite. He wore it almost forty times, Kim revealed, more than Any Other Jumpsuit Ever.

"The Aztecs," Kim informed us, "were Indians." Together with the Romanians, who talked all the time — even when Kim was trying to explain, rather ominously, how all of this would belong to Lisa Marie one day, one day soon "when she can do with it as she pleases"—I saw Elvis's living room. It had a white plush carpet. The white plush sofa had white plush throw pillows to match.

"Oh my God!" a woman from Cleveland screamed to her husband, who was wearing a beret. "These are our colors!

"We should have seen this before we did the hall. Look at the mirrors. *We* could have had mirrors."

There were mirrors in the TV room too. It had three sets, so that Elvis could be just like the president and watch all three networks at one time, Kim said. The TV room had mirrors halfway up the walls. The woman from Cleveland said it reminded her somehow of Robert Goulet.

Kim, however, was urging us on to the racquetball court. There, Kim told us, Elvis had played two strenuous games of racquetball on the sweltering mid-August morning of his death. The last song he ever sang was "Unchained Melody," Kim said. She did not mention The Commode.

She said we should move outside to the Meditation Garden, where no smoking was allowed but where we could take as many pictures as we liked. We could even use a flash. We could pause there as long as we desired, Kim said. Shuttle buses would be running to the parking lot every ten minutes. There was no need to rush.

"Do you see those big kettles around the fountain?" a blond woman in an Oleg Cassini sweatshirt asked one of the Romanians. "Those are the eternal flames.

"They're not burning now," she explained, "because it's off-season."

The Romanian explained this, in turn, to his friend. Everybody else stood around and tried to read the epitaphs. Even in off-season, there were fresh flowers everywhere. People had brought them from as far away as Cleveland. Even in off-season, the epitaphs were copyright 1977. The copyright was cast right there in the bronze so that Vernon Presley's poem about his son Elvis could not turn up uncredited in a perpetual-care lot somewhere in Cleveland—at least not without permission from an Elvis attorney and, one day soon, from Lisa Marie.

People in windbreakers were taking pictures of each other. I got back on the bus. I got a window seat. When we passed through the gates—the big wavelike cast-bronze gates Elvis designed for himself—I could read the Magic Marker inscription on one of the big cast-bronze treble clefs. It said, "I will always love you darling. Velma—1989." It was written for Elvis. It was not written for anyone Velma ever knew.

That night I was sitting in a pale-wood bar in a pale-wood restaurant on a pale-wood eastside Memphis street. I was waiting for a table to open up so that I could eat pasta, in a sauce without any cream. I was having a martini. I was also reading a book. I had spent a day at Graceland. I did not need new friends.

The book was supposed to say all this for me. It did not work.

I heard a voice behind me, a voice that was a curling, smoky squeal. "What are you doing here, reading that book?" the voice asked. A Scotch-glass-clammy hand grazed the back of my neck. A fingernail slid lightly below my collar.

I figured this was someone I knew. I figured it was one of those Memphis former Miss Americas—maybe one who had somehow managed not to marry a doctor. I had met a lot of former Miss Americas. I used to go to Memphis a lot.

I thought it would be somebody I knew. It was not. It was a woman named Rita. Her face was very close to mine and her Scotch-clammy hand was now massaging the back of my gray tweed jacket. She had never been a Miss America. The idea of a doctor, however, had often crossed her mind.

"What are you reading?" she asked. "A biography," I said. "A biography of Barbara Hutton." I used a finger to mark my place, third paragraph down on the right-hand page.

"Is it good," Rita asked, her Scotch hand kneading my tweed-sleeved tricep, "or is it Trash?"

"I guess it's both," I said. "It shows that you can spend a billion dollars in forty years. All you have to do is marry seven husbands, not eat, and end up weighing eighty-six pounds."

"Writers are so wicked," Rita said, positioning her flat-black pageboy behind her ear and peering into the depths of my almost-gone martini. The bartender, leaning against the cash register, stood waiting.

"Be careful what you say about writers," I said. "That's what I do. I write."

"You write?" she squealed, her voice fading like a worn-out smoke ring in the rattling of the pale-wood air. "Would I have read you?"

"Probably not," I said.

"Why not?" she asked. Her face grew hard; she expected a smack.

"I just can't think how it would have happened," I said. Her jaw relaxed.

"This thing you're reading," she said, "this Barbara Hutton thing—I guess it's no *Gone With the Wind*."

"I don't know," I said, trying to find my place on the right-hand page. "She was sort of like a Scarlett O'Hara. Tiny waist; lots of husbands."

"That is just incredible," Rita squealed. "It is just uncanny. That's exactly what my friends all call me. They all call me 'Miss Scarlett.'"

"Somehow, I expected that," I said. Rita smiled. "I hope you have a very nice night," Rita said. I said, "I hope you have a nice night too." Her hand slipped off my shoulder. She winked at the bartender. He winked back. And she was gone.

I figured there was not much point in telling her about Graceland. I figured she had been there before. I figured she had never told anybody, but she had been upstairs. I figured she knew it was off-season for the eternal flames.

The Splendor in the Glass

Please, no plastic corks

A GENTLEMAN DOES not get champagne hangovers. If a gentleman has drunk a great deal of champagne one evening — say, anything more than four bottles, without much help from anyone else — and the next morning his head feels like a bus trip to West Virginia, it must be because he drank something else. It must be because he drank brandy. It must be because the fish course was slightly awry. It must be because he rented his suit.

It cannot be because of the champagne. Champagne is the gentleman's friend.

I like to fancy myself a gentleman: I write thank-you notes and am available to finish out tables. I do not pick up frozen items in the grocery store and then leave them stuffed behind the canned tuna when I discover I have to have toilet paper and I have only $2.46 left to my name. I do not stand around at buffet tables and pick all the cashews out of the mixed nuts. When people call me at 6:32 on a Friday evening and ask me what magazines I read, I do not tell them their parents are dogs.

I have a book to keep up with birthdays. I own two pairs of black lace-up shoes. I do not sit around in wet swimsuits in the summer. And I drink a lot of champagne.

I drink it without excuse or apology. I do not wait for anybody to get married. I do not wait for anybody to give birth.

I drink it when I've finished my laundry and the count on the socks comes out even. I drink it when I get back from the car wash and discover that all four floormats are still there and that my interior does not smell like a piña colada. I drink it when there is an opera on television, and I drink it when there is a rerun of "Night Court."

I drink it when I have just remembered the name of the actress who played the Empress Eugenie opposite Bette Davis in *Juarez*. I drink it when the Cubs win anything, even though I don't have one-clue-in-hell what they play. I drink it when I get a letter from some guy named Robert H. Treller telling me that if I act quickly I can win $40 million and have my name included on computer-generated mailings to 750 million people, right next to some other guy named David Brumbalow from Missoula, Montana. I drink it when I get a magazine with perfume samples. I drink it whenever any two people refuse to name their daughter Brittany. I drink it when anybody in my apartment complex has a cat fixed.

I drink it with salad, and I drink it with dessert. I drink it anytime anyone in the world is eating poached eggs. It has never given me a hangover I care to remember. It has never given me an evening I care to forget.

I knew from my youth just what it would be like. I knew it would not go down bursting like bourbon; it would not sit all coddled against a warm palm. I knew its first sip would crack open into a thousand-white-blue-million pieces, sharp stinging shards glancing straight up to the head. Its bubbles would not burst; they would shatter. Inside they would be all mirrored light.

I knew it would teach me to rhumba; I knew it would make me know Cole Porter songs. I would sing "Night and Day," complete with the verse. I would sing "Easy To Love." I would sing "It's De-Lovely," while my shoes would glide glasslike over polished wood dance floors. My tailcoat would fly out like quick snapping wings. My collar would hold my jaw up and out, strong and jaunty, discovering a dimple cleft deep in my chin. My shirtfront would sparkle with rubies; it would be starched-stiff and bleached-white enough to blind. I would rhumba and cha-cha and foxtrot, and my socks would never slide down.

There are people who drink champagne and do not feel these things. They are people who put it in punch. They drop fruit in it and mix it with orange juice and cranberries and raspberry-syrup liqueur. They serve it in wide-open coupes made for sherbet, so that the bubbles are gone before they ever reach anyone's nose. They sip it slowly and eat wedding cake with icing made mostly of lard. They balance their coupes on the side of glass saucers and talk about having new pins in their hips. Under no circumstances do they ever have a second glass. They do all this and then wonder why they feel ill. They go home when the band plays "Begin the Beguine." In the morning their mouths all taste like glue.

Either that, or they only talk about champagne and save it until New Year's Eve; they make a big deal of it and drink it precisely as midnight turns twelve. They drink one bottle that they share among something like eighteen people. It is a bottle that they have been saving for the past eleven-and-a-half months. It has a plastic cork, and they serve it in little coupe glasses too. People have one measly sip and begin to get kissy. In the morning, they do not speak to one another. They do not speak to one another until sometime in March.

These are people who are out of practice. A gentleman, however, knows the drinking of champagne is a strengthening skill. It must be drunk on as many days as possible, to make ready for days of duress. It must be drunk alone, or it must be drunk by loud, high-laughing parties. It must be drunk cold; it must never be drunk flat. It does not have to hold for occasions. It does not even have to wait for the laundry to come back.

A gentleman may drink it in sweats in front of the TV. He can drink it during "Northern Exposure" while Fleischman

and O'Connell are driving each other desperately, achingly
mad. He can drink it with a cold pastrami sandwich, knowing
all the while that he merely takes it in preparation for the day
it will come to him on a tray. He will check his shoes to make
sure they are ready. He will check to make sure he has good
black silk hose.

In the background he will swear he hears Merman. He will
sing along with her. Together, they will sing "You're the Top."
Across the carpet he will do a quick foxtrot. It will be Wednesday, but the night will be all blue-white stars. He will be
dancing and singing Cole Porter. He will be dancing; he will be
holding the air.

Muscle Tension

Given the alternative of a woman like Tina, is
an aneurysm such a horrible thing?

F OUR TIMES a week, I put on a pair of tights and am yelled
at for a solid hour by a very sinewy woman named Tina.
Actually, she is not always the same woman, and her name is
not always Tina. Sometimes it is Kim.

I am not alone in this experience. I am usually surrounded
by nineteen-year-old girls in boxer shorts and T-shirts that
help them remember the time they got Really Drunk in 1991 at
a Mardi Gras party in Tupelo, Mississippi. There are also
several women in leotards designed by the same person who
designs leotards for Leeza Gibbons, and there are a couple of
men in tank tops from a bar outside Ft. Walton Beach. Tina
yells at us all.

She is wearing a headband and shiny silver tights that make
her legs look like they are made of galvanized steel. We attempt
to do what she says. We do not want her to become upset. Tina
has a part-time job. She paper-trains pit bulls. Her success rate
is 100 percent. There is not a mark on her.

With every sinew in her taut torso, every muscle in her gun-
barrel-sleek thighs, Tina is making us better people. Standing
in front of a plate-glass mirror—and squatting with our knees
apart, our abdominals contracted, and our pelvises thrust
forward—each of us is urged to Look Inside and See the
Person We Want To Become. This process requires that we

close our eyes. Clearly, the Person We Are Right Now is not what Tina has in mind. She closes her eyes too.

Tina knows that each of us is there for his or her own reasons: She knows that some of us are there to relieve the stress of our high-powered jobs. She knows that others of us are there to maximize the efficiency of our cardiovascular systems. She knows that still others of us are there to improve our general attitudes toward the complex challenges known as modern life.

Basically, however, she knows that the girls in the boxer shorts are there because they're afraid they will look Really Fat and end up dating education majors. The women in the leotards are there because they're afraid they will look Really Fat and end up dating Amway salesmen. And the men in tank tops are there because they're afraid they will look Really Fat and end up having to date somebody else who is Really Fat too.

My personal reasons for being there are far more simple: I have this pair of yellow pants. They are all cotton—fully lined—and I haven't been able to get into them since 1982. When I put them on, I look Really, Really Fat.

That is why I do this. It is what I call Working Out. I chose it because it has nothing to do with catching things or picking up objects weighing approximately as much as the state of Minnesota. It does not require grunting.

I chose it because it only requires that I count to four and be able to pick up a boxstep without too much trouble. I chose it because I knew the words to almost all of Little Richard and basically everything by The Supremes. I figured I would be qualified for advanced placement. I chose it because I am a man who satisfied his college phys-ed requirement with two hours in fly-and-bait casting and something called Leisure Time Activities, also known as Advanced Rook.

I had not counted on Tina. In college, Tina took courses like Introduction to Mindless Cruelty, Basic Abrasiveness, and Elementary Tortures of the Damned. In the latter, she was a student assistant.

She has transformed her body into a glistening machine, fueled entirely by complex carbohydrates and mineral water that does not fizz. Her existence is meted out in counts of eight. Everything she does with her left leg she repeats with her right. The search for improved arch support consumes her waking hours.

The contents of her lingerie drawer consist of seventeen jogging bras. She wears them on dates.

Most of the time, Tina is hoarse from yelling at girls in boxer shorts and men in souvenir tank tops from Florida. This means that her voice is now softened to a sultry, smoke-kissed sort of huskiness that men who drink beer find intriguing. They think they are getting Ingrid Bergman. What they are getting is Paul Bear Bryant with a wine glass full of bottled water.

These beer-drinking persons, of course, have never experienced Tina's floorwork. They have never seen the way her triceps bulge and quiver when she does her lateral raises. They know nothing of the way she gets this cute little dimple in her left buttock when she flexes her bicep femoris. They have never seen her reduce grown men to tears.

They can have no inkling that they are in the presence of a woman whose favorite joke is, "Let's do our sit-ups now. Four hundred ninety-nine, 498. . . ." They can scarcely comprehend the terror of a woman who begins her classes by warning: "If anybody here has back trouble, or if anybody's had recent abdominal surgery, I want them to be REALLY careful."

Yet this is a woman who sees me four times a week in black Capri-length tights—tights in which I look like an extra from a bad Ann-Margret movie. This is a woman at whose bidding I do the can-can and something known as "The Monkey Jerk" to selections from the *Honeymoon in Vegas* sound track. This is a woman whom I pay good money to remind me that the gluteus maximus is the largest muscle in my lower body.

I hope her headband hurts.

A Mind Is a Terrible Thing

If you're really smart, James Fenimore Cooper does not have to destroy your life

I WAS A CHILD of privilege. The book-mobile parked in my front yard. It arrived on the second Tuesday of every month, June, July, and August. It pulled into the drive at 11:30 and sat there for forty-five minutes. It sat there for me to use. I knew it was something other children did not have. I did not tell other children when it came.

It parked in my driveway because my mother had helped pass the petition that made it possible. She had gotten more names than anyone else in the world.

She had driven her own car around from house to house every afternoon for almost all of an entire Alabama summer. She had carried a red-plaid school-lunchbox thermos of ice water in the floorboard and a list of addresses printed in pale-purple duplicator ink. The ink on the bottom pages was still slightly damp. If you breathed it in slowly in the gold-uphol-stered stillness of the Rambler's back seat, you could make yourself drunk.

"Stop sniffing the list," my mother would say. "You'll make yourself crazy. Get up here in the front."

"I have to go in here," she said at white people's houses. "Don't play with the brake."

She walked up on white people's porches and knocked hard on their loose front screen doors. She told them her name and told them who she was before she got married. Then she asked them if they wanted the best for their children. She said she was sure they did too. She said she was sure they were worried, as she was, about the brains of tomorrow's grown men. She said children all over the county were wasting a fourth of their lives. She said they were spending too much time at the lake. She had a chart with a pie graph to help her explain.

She held out a clipboard and held out a pen. Then she said Thank You and got back in the car. It took even less time at black people's houses. She rolled down her window and honked the horn until somebody walked out. At black people's houses she did not mention the lake.

My mother got 1,672 names on her petition. The next highest person got something like 32.

The county paid $742 for a used bookmobile they found on a lot. They painted it green, and somebody's father painted library books all over the side. One of them said "Shakespeare," and another one said "Sir Walter Scott." There was "Emerson" and "Dickens" and "Louisa May Alcott" too. They were all in primary colors. Somebody's father had spelled "Louisa May Alcott" with only one *T*.

Inside in the darkness, I looked at the books. I said, "What have you got on opera?"

The bookmobile librarian was having her lunch. It was a piece of cold chicken, a stuffed egg, and a brownie. She had spread out a paper napkin on her collapsible bookmobile counter. She ate with her fingertips and stopped to wipe her lips. She poured lemonade out of a juice jar into a coffee cup. She sipped the lemonade with just the edge of her lips. She asked me, "Mmm?" Her lips left a print on the cup.

I said, "I want to see what there is about opera." I asked her if she could show me where all the opera books were kept.

"No, I don't think so," she said as she tore off a bite of her brownie. "I don't think there's a book about opera on this whole bus."

I said, "Oh."

She said, "We've got Hardy Boys. You could read those in a hurry. Science is the shelf by the window, the one next to the door." She was folding her napkin and pressing it flat to her lips.

She said, "Maybe you could read *The Deerslayer*. Boys like *The Deerslayer* a lot."

I said, "I was really kinda interested in opera."

"I'll check with the county," she said. "I'll write it down for next month." She looked hard at her napkin and redid her lips. She did not have to take her compact out of her purse.

"But I think you ought to check out *The Deerslayer*," she said as she reopened her ink pad and set out her stamps. "It's got Indians, and it's just full of adventure. It's the kind of book little boys love."

I looked up and saw a book about ballet. I did not ask her to help me take it down.

Outside, the bookmobile driver was finishing his smoke break. The bookmobile librarian lady said, "Have you found what you'd like for today?"

I took *Ivanhoe*, *Père Goriot*, and a book on the Lizzie Borden axe-murder case. The bookmobile librarian watched me. I took down *The Deerslayer* too.

"That's a lot of big reading," she said, patting the books into a neat little stack and removing each one's card. "But I know you're smart." She was inking her stamp and stamping each book with a due date, one month away. It was the day the bookmobile came back.

"Now what is it you want to be?" she said as she pushed my books toward me. "Is it a doctor? Is that what you want to be?"

I said, "I want to sing in the opera." She said, "Oh." She said, "You'll have to sing something for me sometime soon." I slid my books off the counter. I held them against my stomach. I wanted to cut out my tongue.

The bookmobile driver was standing in the doorway. The librarian lady handed him a brownie and smiled. She said, "Are there any other little boys and girls coming today?"

I said, "No. I don't think so. My brother's at the IGA working bag-boy. I'm the only one here."

She said, "I want you to call lots of other little boys and girls before we come back next time. This bookmobile is their bookmobile too."

I said, "They're all at the lake."

She said, "Colored children can use the bookmobile too." The bookmobile driver started the bookmobile engine. The bookmobile librarian said, "I want you to tell me about all these books when we come back. You're going to love Natty Bumpo. Next time, I'll bring you *White Fang* or maybe *The Call of the Wild.*"

I said, "Thank you."

She said, "Tell your mother hello." I stepped down from the bookmobile into the driveway. The sunshine hit my eyes. A shard of gravel stung into my barefoot left heel. The smell of the bookmobile diesel fumes itched in my nose.

Inside, the maid was on the back porch ironing. I gave her *The Deerslayer.* I said it was something her boy could read. I said boys like him would like it a lot.

My mother asked me, "Did you get something nice from the bookmobile lady?"

I said I was going to read two books by Jack London. I said the smell of the diesel fuel made me drunk in the heat. I said "Louisa May Alcott" was spelled with two *T*'s.

A Little off the Top

He's wearing a ponytail;
request two I.D.'s

A man in a ponytail will not call back. Women need to know this. They need to understand this before they let men in ponytails start buying the drinks.

Before a woman tells a man in a ponytail that yes-she-will-have-maybe-just-one-more-mai-tai, she needs to understand that he will not be calling the next morning before noon. Before she admits that no-I-never-have-had-an-ouzo-shooter-but-if-you-think-it's-all-right-on-top-of-three-mai-tai's-I-guess-I-could-try-just-one, she needs to understand that he will not remember her phone number. He will lose the slip of paper he wrote it down on. At nine o'clock the next morning, while she is lying by the phone hoping that her head will not explode, he will be trading that slip of paper in for a pair of resoled Italian loafers. In the middle of a game of handball, a half-hour later, it will dawn on him that he cannot remember her last name. In the shower at 10:45, it will dawn on him that he cannot remember her first name either. He will not be too damned sure he ever really asked.

In the shower, he will feel a little guilty. He will turn to somebody else and say, "I met this great woman last night." A man with a ponytail—even a ponytail that is a damp, limp, shower-soggy mess—would never say, "I met this great girl."

Somebody else in the shower will say, "Great, where'd you meet her?"

The guy with the ponytail will say, "I bought her some drinks. We had a great time."

Somebody else will say, "Great, what's her name?" The guy with the ponytail will say, "Beats the hell out of me. Is that your shampoo?"

At home, the woman will be looking for an ice pack. She will remember his name very well. His name will be Brock. She will be leaning against her microwave and chanting, "Brock, Brock, Brock, Brock, Brock, Brock, Brock."

The phone will ring and she will trip in her pine-scented kitty box trying to answer before he hangs up. Her whole kitchen will smell like a great fresh knotty-pine forest before she can get to the phone.

She will wait for three rings because she figures that will make her look calm. When she picks up the receiver, it will be her friend, Trudy. Trudy will say, "What's wrong with you?"

She will scrape the fresh-as-all-outdoors kitty litter from between her toes and say, "Nothing. Why do you ask?"

Trudy will say, "You waited for the third ring. You must have been expecting a guy."

She will say, "Trudy, I met this beautiful boy." Trudy will say, "What do you mean, you met a boy?" She will say, "He looked just like a boy. He had all this beautiful hair."

Trudy will say, "What else do you remember?" She will say, "He pulled his hair back. He wore it in a ponytail, and his name was Brock."

Trudy will say, "Fix yourself an ice pack. I'll be right there."

A woman who meets a man in a ponytail does not have to put herself through this degree of pain. She should have one weak Scotch-and-water and then drive herself home. He is, after all, a man in a ponytail. A man with long hair — Long Hair He Ties Back.

It is long hair he can wear at the bank. It is long hair he can wear with a suit. It is long hair that is not really long hair at all

It is long hair that is short when people see him from the front. It is long hair that is only long hair when he is leaving a room. If he does not turn his head sideways, no one will know. If he wears one gold earring, it will have a screwpost on the back. If he has a tattoo, it is on his right hip. If he pays to live anywhere, he rents. He has never sent flowers in his life.

He is a man terrified by commitment. He wants to have long hair, but he is not really quite sure. He saw long hair once on a lean Italian model in a $28 magazine with a text entirely in French. But he also saw it this morning on three guys on a work crew wearing hardhats with their butts hanging out of their jeans. He has seen these things, and they have made him unsure. They have made him want to tie his hair back.

His hairdresser has told him, if he ties his hair back, it will highlight his structure. He has told him it will look great for the fall. He has said it will touch him with mystery. He has told him it does not make him look gay, not even one bit at all.

What he has not told him is that it makes him look like Grace Kelly in a 42-long. What he has not told him is that most men who wear ponytails are required to do so because there are laws to protect us from finding hair in our food. What he has not told him is that he is going to go bald in about three weeks and have to have plugs.

Right now, however, he is thinking about his cheekbones and the way they will look all angled when his hair is pulled tight back. Right now, he is wondering if he can work a whole day without turning sideways to anybody at the bank. Right now, he is wondering what women who like ponytails will drink. Right now, he is wondering if his Speedo would hide a little heart-shaped tattoo.

But a woman drinking mai-tai's does not know these things. She figures he plays in a band and has written a screenplay for a movie starring Harrison Ford. She thinks his ponytail expresses a slight vulnerability. She thinks it makes him look like a wide-eyed, sharp-cheekboned, slightly balding little boy. When he talks, he turns his head sideways a lot.

One Monday, right in the middle of lunch, my friend Gretchen the graphic artist asked me to think seriously about ponytails. I was having turkey and Swiss, side order of slaw; she was having corned beef, bag of chips, because she wanted red meat. She was also having a beer. She had to drink almost half of it before she could get the question out.

"I mean, what do you think of men wearing ponytails?" she said as she shuffled through her chips. "Sometimes, I think it can look just really cool."

I said, "I don't know. I think it makes your hair fall out."

Gretchen said, "Maybe. I figure a guy with a ponytail has got to be deep down really actually kinda sweet."

I said, "Why do you think that?" "I don't know," said Gretchen, who had lighted a cigarette and was staring beyond me into the chalkboard, where a sandwich guy with a ponytail was erasing the specials of the day. "I met this guy with a ponytail just the other night. He had these great cheekbones, and, when he pulled his hair back, it made his eyes look really, really sad."

I said, "He probably had a headache. I hear that's what happens when you tie your hair back. I hear sometimes you can't remember anything at all."

I said, "Do you want another beer?" Gretchen said, "No," and looked down at her napkin. She said, "I think I have to go now. I have to give Trudy a call."

Blood Sport

Memories of the good life, au jus

 I THINK I remember red meat. Sometimes, in fact, I think I remember it rather fondly. I am sure it must be some sort of man thing. I am sure it must have something to do with hormones.

Once in a while, however, the memory of medium-rare hamburger meat will come over me, all unannounced and uninvited. I will be doing bicep curls with a pair of forty-five-pound hand weights, and I will remember the taste of blood in my mouth. I will remember biting through a charred crust of meat crunch, my teeth sliding slickly into a slab of still-pink, just-warm flesh. I will remember the juices and the chewing and the ketchup and the slice of cheese, melted into a sheet of satin and slipping down like a piece of lingerie over the edge of the bun. I will remember the smokiness that hung in my mouth and could be washed away with nothing but beer. I will remember the way the lazy smokiness mixed in with the burned-grain angst of the beer until, together, they made a soft, cool-burning slosh in my throat. I will remember these things and feel the need to do triceps and 178 push-ups. I will go to the showers and let the water run hot and hard over my body for a very long time.

These days, however, I live a life in which red meat is mostly a memory. In restaurants I cannot even find it on menus. At dinner parties, I am offered only chicken and fish, since veal would be horrid and inhuman and one never knows who will eat pork. I am promised that I need only bring white wine because we will be having something light, with maybe a scoop of sorbet or a little fruit and some sliced-up avocado that will have to pass for a salad. Again and again, I am guaranteed that, after dinner, I will not feel stuffed. I do not dare admit that the thought of a full stomach would not deeply disturb me. I figure, all I can do is pray there will be a sauce on the grouper. If there is not, I figure I can eat all the bread.

I have learned to accept this sort of white-meat imitation of life. I have learned to eat raw fish and pasta with odd-colored, pine-nut-flavored sauces and chicken breasts soaked in peppers that scald and blister my tongue's tender scalp. I have learned to accept all these diversionary tactics, these desperate efforts to approximate dinner, these nervous attempts to keep our minds off red meat. I have eaten them like a three-pack-a-day smoker chewing gum on an airplane. I have uncomplainingly accepted them like a sworn-off-martinis drinker sipping Perrier and aching for gin. I have come to grips with them in the same way leaden-souled couples come to grips with a bad marriage in which children are involved. I have learned to believe such things are real dinners, just as I have learned to believe real suntans can come out of a tube.

I am fully convinced that there are indeed individuals in this world who feel that they are better people because they do not put red meat in their mouths. They feel that their feet somehow tread the earth's surface more lightly because they bring their own tofu burgers to company cook-outs. They are confident that they have saved an acre of Venezuelan rain forest every time they make a dinner entirely from beans.

Standing around at pool parties, wearing flat shoes and drinking mineral water that has been ordered without ice cubes, they explain that they do not feel animosity against the meat-eating world. On the contrary, they maintain that they do not feel any animosity against any living, breathing thing on this earth. They have not, in fact, been angry or shaved any part of their bodies, they explain, since some time in 1978, when, for the first time, they really listened to what James Taylor was saying.

They watch a couple of gnats having sex in their mineral water and they say that, since they have quit eating Big Macs, they are merely at peace with small insects and most blooming plants. They reveal that, for them, each day's sunrise is now a moment of exquisite, almost surreal, calmness. Every breath they breathe is a prayer of gratitude to the green photosynthetic source of life. They are humbled, they explain, even by the sight of a hearty growth of privet hedge. Then they look deep into a space that is somewhere behind the back of your eyes and ask if you would like to have a Swedish massage. They ask if you know where they could get some good dope.

At such moments, I generally lie. I tell such people that I never think about eating red meat anymore; I tell them just a little piece of fish and a lemon wedge is all I require on most nights. I tell them I think a massage would be lovely. I tell them I like their shoes. I tell them I do not know anybody who ever smokes dope.

All the while, I am remembering Sunday afternoons with platters of country-fried steak, battered heavy and served up with French fries. I am remembering Saturday nights with full-pound slabs of juice-oozing sirloin and baked potatoes the size of my head. I am remembering burgers and prime rib and London broil and stews and roast beef sandwiches sharp with mustard and marbleized with fat. I am remembering the way I would eat these things and lie down for hours of heavy, blood-rich dreams of depravity and power and lust. I would eat these things, as I remember it, and for days my feet would make deep, heavy tracks in the earth. I would knot my hands into fists and feel the desire to punch strangers straight in the mouth. I would consider belching in public and volunteering for the Army Reserves.

At dinner parties now, I do not raise these sorts of memories. I live a calm-eyed, clean-veined, salt-free, and bloodless existence. I lift hand weights and jump off buildings on bungee cords to rid myself of these memories. At dinner, I eat what I am served.

Someone to Watch over Me

Two pictures of Mary
are all I have left

T HIS IS NOT a story about my mother. It is a story about
somebody else. It is about a woman who used to pick me
up and carry me around on her hip. Her name was Mary, and
I do not know where she is now.

My mother did not pick up children. My mother had a bad
back. If she could have picked up children, she would have; but
my mother had soft bones. She had such soft bones that she had
to drink a glass of milk at every meal. When she was pregnant,
the doctor had ordered her to eat chalk. He had ordered her to
eat big sheets of it. It was prescription chalk, and she bought it
at the drugstore to make sure that it was clean.

Three times a day, from the day the doctor had informed her
that there was no chance she was anything else but pregnant,
she would eat a piece of chalk. She would chew it until it had
formed a thick wad of mush in her mouth. Even though she
would try to wash it down with a bottled Coca-Cola, it still
scratched the sides of her throat with a dry, grainy dust. She
would chew it slowly in an attempt not to choke. Even with
deep drafts from the flat Coca-Cola, on every mouthful of chalk
she would gag.

My mother told us about the chalk-sheets a lot. In later
years, when my brother was old enough to form complete
sentences, he would say, "God, Mama, that is so gross." My

mother would say, "I did this to give you life. Do not take the Lord's name in vain."

Because she had soft bones, my mother could not pick up children. She would allow them to crawl up into her lap, even though she swore she had no lap at all. When children perched on the edge of her knee, she would read them stories. Sometimes, she would tell them about the chalk too.

This story, however, is not about my mother. It is about Mary, who came every day to pick children up. Almost everything I know about her is something I know from a picture. Everything I remember about her from life is all wrong.

I remember her walking up the driveway to the house in the low blue-gold glare of an Alabama early morning. I remember her wearing a gray starched cotton uniform with a sweater to match. I remember that her shoulders were broad, just like my own mother's shoulders. I remember that, when she walked, she lifted her black leather shoes so that they did not stir the dust. I remember that her hair was a thick shiny-black mass.

I remember that I ran alongside her and she told me not to kick up the dirt. I remember that she said she had to wear her dress all of that day and she didn't want it dirty before she got to the door. I remember that she asked me if I had had my breakfast. I remember she asked me if I had drunk my juice.

I remember her, later that afternoon, in the living room. I remember that she is sitting deep in an overstuffed, chenille-crusty armchair, while I am rolling wild in the middle of the living-room rug. I remember that she is helping me play.

I know, however, that I have seen Mary in pictures. There are only two of these pictures, but they tell me that, in all I remember, there is nothing that is possibly true.

In one of the pictures, my brother and I are wearing sunsuits. We are with Mary, and we are in the side yard. My mother is taking the picture. Her shadow falls out broad on the grass. In the background there is a barbed wire fence. The fence means there are cows.

It is my first birthday, and I am sucking on two right-hand fingers. Mary has pulled a kitchen chair out into the yard dirt, and she is sitting down and holding me tight to her in the rounded crook of her smooth right arm. With her left arm she is gripping my brother, who is struggling and picking his nose. Mary is looking meekly up into the camera. Her hair is a soft fuzzy scraggle of braids. She is probably sixteen years old. None of us is wearing shoes, and Mary has gripped her toes around a rung of the chair. She is wearing a loose-buttoned housedress that does not seem to have much color at all. This is my favorite picture of Mary.

In the other picture, Mary is washing a dog while my brother and I stand around watching and pretending to help. We are all a year older, and I can stand up by myself. The dog's name is Droopy, and this is the last picture taken of him before he disappeared out of our lives. My mother explained later that she was sure that, one day, somebody passing by had opened a car door and Droopy had jumped in. She said Droopy never met a stranger. She said, if somebody had hit him, she was sure we would have heard the crash.

Now, however, Droopy is covered in detergent soapsuds. Mary is lifting him out of the washtub so that he holds his head up for the camera. She is holding him so that he is crossing his paws. The front of her dress has been stained dark with the water, and there are suds dripping off her short, shining arms. My brother and I are wearing matching shirt-and-short sets. My brother is raising a scrub brush directly over Mary's head. In the struggle to hold Droopy in his pose for the camera, she is straining and biting her tongue.

If I want to, I can remember part of that moment with Mary, except that I remember that her arms were slender and long. I can remember my mother trying to focus the camera, then stopping to smooth the curve of my white-baby-blond hair. I can remember that we went into the kitchen to drink lemonade. If I try very hard, I can remember Mary standing in the door

leading onto the back porch, drinking lemonade from a glass
that she kept by the sink.

The next year we got a TV and saw Lucille Ball for the first
time. The year after that, we moved, and I cannot think that I
ever saw Mary again. Every week, a tall black woman with
tightly plaited hair came to the house to do ironing. When there
was news about Rosa Parks on the TV, my mother said we
should turn it off. My mother said we should not make noise
and bother the ironing woman, whose name was Ola. She said
I was too big by then to need to be picked up.

She said I was too big by then to remember much about
Mary at all. My mother said, "Mary wasn't anything at all like
Ola. She loved you boys as if you were her own. The day we
moved, she looked like she was going to cry." Mary had packed
all the boxes, and she had dropped a figurine. My mother had
glued it back together and put it on the mantel, but you could
still see the cracks.

I tried hard, but I told my mother I could not remember any
of that. I told her what I was sure I could remember was Mary
drinking her lemonade, standing in the back porch door, using
the glass that she kept by the sink. Anything else, I figure, is
something I have had to make up.

The Thumbs Are Green

A soulful return to the earth

 IT IS SPRING, and people are buying dirt. They are buying bags of it and putting it in the trunks of their beige automobiles and taking it home. Some of them, who do not think the trunks of their beige automobiles are remotely large enough to satisfy their dirt-purchasing needs, are even buying large butch-black, standard-transmission vehicles with a spare tire on the back door, just so they will not have to make two trips to the dirt store.

These people feel good about their dirt. They stand around and talk about it with other people while they are all standing in the dirt-store parking lot on a perfectly pool-appropriate Saturday morning when they could be making pink drinks in a blender and getting a start on their tans. Instead, they are standing around in the heat and talking about dirt while a weekend-help person from the dirt store is loading fifty-pound bags of it into the back of their $37,000 vehicles, each of which has a car phone and a built-in CD player, each of which has a remote-control garage-door opener on the flip-down visor, each of which still has plastic bags on the floormats, each of which is referred to as "The Truck."

47

It is a Saturday, and it is already hot as hell. The dirt people, however, are wearing all the clothes they can possibly find. They are wearing already-old, sort-of-green polo shirts they have ordered from a catalog that sells only dirt-people things. They are wearing khaki pants with kneepads and big saggy unisex bottoms that the catalog promises will give them room when they move. Some of them have even ordered hats and bandannas. They wear the hats cocked at a jaunty, sun-challenging angle and the bandannas in a knot around their necks. Some of them have even ordered gloves as well. Most of them, however, have kept their shoes from last year.

All in all, they have spent something like $42,000, just so they can buy bags of dirt. The dirt itself costs something like $72.50. They tell themselves $72.50 is really not a lot. Not when they consider the quality they are getting. Not when they consider the pleasure it brings.

They do not, after all, consider the dirt they have purchased to be dirt any longer at all. It is in a bag now, so that, now, it is a magical thing. Most of them now call it Soil. Some of them even call it Earth. The very words make their voices grow all shaky and trembly. When they try to explain the depth of their emotion, their throats grow dry and tight.

They talk a lot—in their trembling, dry-throaty voices— about the feel of the soil in their hands. They talk a lot about the joy of getting the earth under their nails. They talk a lot about getting back to their roots. They talk a lot about being at peace. They talk a lot about whether their cordless phones can get a clear signal way out in the garden. They talk a lot about how, if they didn't have their beepers in an economy like this one, they figure they just couldn't live.

Over a brisk little midmorning jolt of espresso, served in itsy-bitsy white china cups at the dirt store's crisp little green-awninged cafe, they confess to one another that they have learned to treat the earth with new reverence. As they spread butter on their croissants, they reveal that the things they are to put into the earth now are far too holy to be merely called

Plants. Brushing the croissant crumbs from their shirtfronts, they gaze off into the traffic-light glittering distance and explain that, as soon as they have paid their tabs and have run by the laundry, they will—this very afternoon—proceed to bless the earth with things they now call Perennials and a few things they call Annuals too.

They will learn Latin names that sound like prayers when they say them. They will learn an amazing amount about Big Woody Stems. They will buy books and pamphlets and become authorities on the subject, and nothing will ever be referred to as You-Know-One-of-Those-Red-Things-That-Looks-Sort-of-Like-a-Dog's-Hiney again. Not for as long as they live.

I myself bought a bag of dirt on one of these Saturdays. I bought it because somebody had given me a plant. It had a big purple flower on it, and I thought it might be kind of neat if it didn't die. I thought maybe, if I put it in a pot with some dirt and left it on the patio, it might possibly live. I thought, maybe, if I left it out there long enough, it might even get rained on. I thought this was how Nature did things.

I described my plant to the guy at the dirt store. He said, "Somebody gave you a hydrangea. Have you been sick?"

I told him I liked my hydrangea. I told him it brought back memories of a very special time. I told him I wanted to plant it and see if it would live. I told him, if it didn't, that would be just all right too. I told him I would have my memories just the same.

The guy in the dirt store said, "Hydrangeas can be very hardy. Do you think this is a commitment you're ready to make?"

I told him I thought I would like a clay pot. I said I thought it would look nice with all the green leaves. He said, "You know you'll have to think about drainage and sunlight and about your hydrangea's contrast to the rest of your garden." He said, "Hydrangeas can look very dramatic. They can overwhelm plantings that don't have as much flair."

I told him there wasn't any rest of my garden. I told him all I wanted was to put this plant in a pot so that I could see how long it would take for the damned thing to die.

The guy in the dirt store said, "I think you're going to need a hat."

I told him what I wanted was a clay pot and one bag of dirt. He said the smallest bag he had was twenty-five pounds. He said it would cost $17.92, tax included. He said he would be glad to have someone load it for me. He said I could bring my truck around.

I did not tell him I had a gray Mazda—with four doors and a dent in the roof. I told him, "No thank you. I'll just load my dirt for myself."

He said, "We have a hydrangea group starting on Thursdays. You might like it. Hydrangea people have so much to share."

That afternoon, I discovered the pool wasn't open. So I sat on the patio and put my plant in a pot. I left it there and waited for rain. It didn't rain until the next Thursday, by which time my plant had turned brown. I have not bothered yet to unpot it. I do not have anything to put in its place.

It will probably be there sometime next winter. A wind will come, and its leaves will fall off. I will look at those leaves and remember. I will figure Nature is a wonderful thing.

A Grown Woman

Coming of age with Jackie O.

I CONFESS THAT, in 1960, the first time I actually remember seeing a Kennedy, I probably didn't have a very firm grip on reality. But then, neither did the rest of the nation.

I had an excuse—I was only ten years old and had never been farther north than Huntsville. I wore penny loafers because I still couldn't tie my shoes. My life revolved around Carl Betz and Donna Reed. I read "Dondi" in the funnies every Sunday and wanted desperately to be an orphan.

I had never seen anybody who was Catholic—except for one time when I saw three nuns in a hospital and my mother told me to stop asking questions. I had never seen a black person sit down in a restaurant. I had never seen a president with a full head of hair.

These, however, were merely my excuses. The rest of the nation had some explaining to do.

In 1960, the rest of the nation thought of itself as Pretty Neat. As far as the rest of the nation was concerned, nobody really important was at war. The rest of the nation honestly believed that, if you put your head under your desk, you could survive a nuclear holocaust. The rest of the nation thought there really was something going on between Rock Hudson and Doris Day.

We—all of us, me and the rest of the nation—watched "American Bandstand" and ate red M&M's. And then we saw the Kennedys.

There were a lot of them, and they were all young and very tan. Whenever they smiled, they showed their teeth. They all had lots of teeth, and they smiled easily—the way people smile when they've spent all their summers in family compounds on The Cape. The way people smile when they expect everybody they see to be either a retainer or a first cousin once removed.

The look of them had nothing to do with Hollywood. Their hair was not blond, and they wrinkled easily. They wore Brooks Brothers suits that hung on them like sacks. They seemed very different from the rest of us, and yet they seemed real.

They looked like they owned things—because they did. They clearly did not worry about car payments or whether they could afford to brick in the patio this summer. They moved easily, like young lions—more than cubs but not yet fully maned and grizzled—moving together in a pride. Sometimes, when they did not get their way, their faces grew stern. Their smiles grew hard.

They could wait out anything. They were young. And in their midst there was Jackie.

She was not a Kennedy woman. Kennedy women were ruddy-skinned. Their hair was sunstreaked, and they had big teeth. Their teeth showed when they smiled. Jackie never really smiled at all. When she tried smiling—in the middle of a yardful of autoworkers, maybe, or trapped at a head table beside some senior senator from a Southern state—she only managed to look sad.

She was large-eyed and beautiful. She was younger even than the Kennedys, but the look of her hurt. She was, in a word, perfect.

Among all those lions, she was a doelike creature. She liked being with her children, she wore pearls, and she never raised her voice. Nobody dared yell at her in public. She had about her the solemnity of Jennifer Jones in *The Song of Bernadette;* yet when she spoke she sounded, with a ghastly irony, like Marilyn Monroe.

Everything about her was careful; everything was elegant. But nothing was exactly at ease. When she went to the White House, all across the country Nice Girls with Quiet Good Taste crossed their ankles and smiled a gentle, satisfied smile of vindication. Jackie was one of theirs. She was no Mamie Eisenhower — she could never have shopped at a PX. And she was certainly no Eleanor Roosevelt — she knew how to wear hats. She was June Cleaver triumphant. She had no cause except the cause of Pretty Things.

With her marriage to John Kennedy, the Sixties and the Fifties had become man and wife. Jack slept around and coped as best he could with Cuba, Kruschev, and the governor of Alabama. Jackie stayed home, redid the White House, and championed a young hatmaker named Halston. If the Kennedy men dreamed of Camelot, the gown of Guinevere tempted her not at all. She did not push.

She had done nothing to deserve the horrors of that November day in Dallas. In its aftermath, the press looked for signs of towering grief, perhaps some glimpse of a Mary Todd Lincoln crumbling into madness. Instead, they got a thirty-four-year-old woman, widowed with two children — a woman who wore dark glasses and sued paparazzi who photographed her eating ice cream.

She opened no drug rehabilitation centers. She joined no Freedom Marches. She was not named ambassador to anything. She did not date Mick Jagger. She did not attempt to become an actress or read poetry aloud in public. Her only memoir recalled a postcollege summer spent with her sister in Europe.

She did not take to making acidic public statements about the Republicans. She did not try to become Alice Roosevelt Longworth. Still, the less Jackie did, the more her fascination grew. The aloof ordinariness that had once been her marvel now became her mystique.

So she married one of the world's richest men — a man given to destroying opera divas and the daughters of men even richer than himself — and, ere long, she was quite a wealthy woman in her own right. Now she could let the cameras snap all they wanted. Now she could be as ordinary as she pleased.

Now she is somewhere in the middle of her sixties. An entire generation knows her only as an Onassis — as a very rich woman who was once married to a President, a woman who edits books, a woman whose son may one day run for the Senate. But even now I remember the sight of her on that blister-cold Inauguration Day of 1961 — when, even to school-children in Alabama, she promised something bright and brilliant for the world.

These days, I fear, the world is much more real than it was two or three decades ago. Chernobyl and Bosnia and AIDS and three Rambo movies have taken a lot of the fun out of life. These days, when Jackie is seen on magazine covers, she has learned how to smile. Sometimes, it is a hard smile — a smile like the Kennedys.

These days, I do not wonder about her life any longer. These days, when I go to the office, I always wear lace-up shoes.

Getting a Buzz

Make it black —who needs sleep?

 THE FIRST TIME I saw a cup of coffee I wanted one. At the time, I was strapped into a chair so that I would not fall into the grits, and I had just spit up some strained bananas on my bib. I was beating on my little tray table with a Howdy Doody spoon and thinking, "Dear God, let me get my training pants this week." I was reaching for my Peter Rabbit Never-Tipsy Juice Cup with the Safe-for-Sipping Lip my mother could never get quite clean, reminding myself all the while, "If I drink one more drop of this stuff, I'm gonna stay in diapers until I get my driver's license."

At the same time, I was thinking, "Hey, what's your problem? You've got two teeth in, and every time you make go-poo-poo, somebody rubs your butt with power." I was thinking, "You're facing a day in which the big crisis is going to be getting down for your two-thirty nap." I was thinking this was not, in short, one damn half-bad life.

Then I saw my father. He was holding a mug of coffee between his palms. He was rolling the mug back and forward so that the heat soaked into his hands. In the mug, the coffee was so black-shiny that it caught fluorescent light and bounced it back off the yellow kitchen walls. It was so hot that it steamed my father's glasses up and sent a comfortable little cloud of fog-warmness up into the seven-o'clock morning air.

I watched my father raise the mug, with both hands, to his mouth. He held it there a long time and felt the steam stinging sharp on his skin. He closed his eyes and breathed the smell of it in, filling his lungs with its burn. When he drank, he made a little slurping noise so that the shiny black razor did not scar his tongue. He took one shy little slurp, and I saw his whole body go tense. Than he took another slurp, and I saw his shoulders relax. He took a third slurp, and I'll swear he fell limp in his chair and went "A-a-a-h."

On the counter the percolator went blip-blurp-blop. On the stove the bacon in the skillet made a crackling noise. When my father drank his coffee, he closed his eyes so that, for the moment, he was away and alone and did not have to sell cars.

In an instant, I hated my apple juice. I looked down at my juice cup and sent it sailing across the room in a banana-mulch spray. My spoon glanced off the dish drainer, and my bowl went clattering to the floor. I sent up the howl of a heart wailing for that first hand slap of caffeine. I wanted that cup of coffee more than all the games of This-Little-Piggy in the world. Maybe I was going to have to grow up to get it, but I did not care. I would do anything; I would even turn two. I wanted that cup of coffee. Just as, oh dear God, I want it now.

For a while I had it. It was, in fact, pretty much the only reason I agreed to puberty. Somehow, I knew, the onset of bad skin would seal me from the world of Peter Rabbit Never-Tipsy Juice Cups forevermore. One morning, I knew, my mother would say, "What's that on your forehead?" Then she would say, "How do you take it—black?" That afternoon, I would come home, and my stuffed Winky Dink Sleepy Pal would have disappeared. That evening at sunset, my father would take me into the back yard for a talk. That night, I would sit in front of the television, stretch my feet out on the gold Barcalounger footrest, and let one last mug of coffee roar its mind-clearing way through my veins. Then I would rest. I would be a man.

I did not get the talk with my father. But I did get my own mug. Over the next twenty-five years, in fact, I got something like 172 mugs, if I am counting correctly: I got mugs with music notes and mugs with cars. I got mugs from banks and mugs from art museums. I got mugs with jokes about cows and mugs with poems by a lady in Philadelphia who believed that each day was better than the one gone before. I got mugs shaped like human skulls and mugs shaped like things for which my mother could not even make up names.

I drank coffee at 6:30 before I got into the shower. I drank it in my car and splashed it on my suitpants on the way to work. I drank it in the copy room while my secretary opened the mail. I drank it at 10:47 because the morning needed a break. I drank it after lunch to get the taste of the pizza sub out of my mouth. I drank it at 3:18 when the afternoon needed a spin. I drank it at 5:13 because I got home and the Neiman's bill had come. I drank it at dinner, and I drank it with dessert. I drank it in front of the TV. I drank it in bed with a book. I envied Carol Lawrence, who could lock herself in a study and drink it to get away from Robert Goulet. I had a silver-haired fantasy involving Mrs. Olsen, Joe DiMaggio, and a can of Folger's drip. I honestly believed Cicely Tyson could drink straight dark French Roast and never get the shakes.

I had slept maybe twenty-six minutes between 1978 and 1984, but I did not care. I figured grown men do not need naps. Grown men need to be alert, ready to attack and grip their opponents with orangy-brown stained teeth. I figured decaf should be a controlled substance. A big mug of real java, however, was to beverages what the missionary position was to sex. Illustrated guidebooks were not required. It was available and easy to do. Our very natures proclaimed it was right. If anybody used a cup for any other purpose, I figured, they should get five-to-seven and have to be surgically fixed.

Then, one day in about 1987, my urologist said, "You can roll over now," and gave me a prescription for apple juice. He told me all about it—how it was refreshing and high in fiber and great for The System of a Guy My Age. He said I should probably start drinking the stuff if I ever wanted to have an erection again.

I drink a lot of apple juice now. But it is not what I asked out of life. I do not think this is one of life's fairer trades. I want a cup of coffee. I want to hold the mug against my palms and let the heat of it heal me up from my hands. I want it so strong it makes my right eyelid twitch. I want it so thick it makes me lie awake until dawn and think of wonderful things.

I do not want a safety juice mug. I do not want to sleep at night. I want a cup of coffee. I want it hot. I want it black. I want it now. On that morning so many years ago, I swear I only threw my juice cup across the kitchen because I thought I wanted to grow up. I did not ask to get old.

Goodnight, Sweetheart, Goodnight

Slow dancing under
the time clock moon

IN MY ENTIRE high school career, I only knew two girls who did not have dates for the prom. One of them had breasts; the other did not.

The girl with breasts was Rhonda Fay Potts. She had had her breasts for a long time — since the summer before seventh grade. On her first day in junior high school, she and the other girls had gone to phys ed. The other girls had not spoken a civil word to her in the five-and-a-half years since.

In tenth grade, when Rhonda Fay Potts went out for cheerleader, she did her windmill jumps and people laughed. Boys talked about her a lot, but she never had dates.

The girl without breasts was named Katinka Freddleman, who was a Lutheran. She was not from a family anyone knew, and she was the only Lutheran anybody in South Central Alabama had ever seen. She kept her hair in place with bobby pins. No one had ever heard her speak.

She looked like she should be smart, but she was not. Somebody said she had older parents, and she always wore socks.

We were all seniors together, and we were supposed to have dates for the prom. In homeroom we were reminded that the prom was a tribute to our achievements and a night we would cherish for the rest of our lives. The homeroom teacher announced that, if they wanted to, boys could wear sports coats and feel perfectly all right. She also read a memo from one of the basketball coaches, who said that the court had just been refinished and asked that the girls not wear spikes.

The people who were not going steady were the only ones who had any cause for concern. In homeroom during the announcements, Rhonda Fay Potts crossed her legs and flipped the pages of a new *Mademoiselle*. Once in a while, when she found a picture of a new hairdo, she would take out a mirror and look at herself. She would use a hair-fluffy brush to tease out a spot in her bangs. Then she would put her mirror back.

The homeroom teacher, who mostly taught typing, would tell her, "Rhonda Fay Potts, do I have to remind you that this is the Secretarial Arts Career Laboratory? It is not the ladies' room." Rhonda Fay Potts would give her shoulders a quick little hoist that made her Peter-Pan-collar-bloused bosoms heave out over her desk. Then she would adjust her left bra strap and begin to clean the hair out of her brush. The girls who went steady would roll their eyes and look up at their boyfriends. Their boyfriends would look down at the floor.

Meanwhile, Katinka Freddleman wore a sweater and smiled out into the air. She sat with her palms placed calmly in front of her, her fingers lightly gripping her chemistry book's edge. Katinka Freddleman wore glasses, but she was repeating chemistry because, when she took it the first time, the best she could do was a *D*.

When the bell rang for first period, the typing teacher said, "Katinka, would you mind waiting behind?" Katinka stood next to the mimeograph machine and waited. She pulled her sweater up tight on her shoulders and held her chemistry book close to her chest.

The typing teacher said, "I wondered what you were doing on prom night. I'm going to chaperone, and I thought, if you'd like to, you could ride with me. It's going to be something beautiful. I think it's something you should see."

Katinka cocked her head at an angle and gave a sweet little meaningless smile. The typing teacher said, "Why don't you check it out with your parents? If you'd like, I could call them at home."

Katinka cocked her head in the other direction so that her gaze drifted mildly away to the shorthand-alphabet chart. The typing teacher said, "Just tell your parents I'll call them tonight. I'll tell them we're having girls' night out." Katinka made a weepy little laugh-sound and arched her eyebrows in a limp little line. One of her bobby pins rattled down to the floor.

Outside in the hall, Katinka stopped beside the radiator to pull up her socks. Rhonda Fay Potts glanced at her for a second from behind the door of her book locker, where she had had a mirror installed. She was squinting into the mirror now and doing her lips. When the second bell rang, she dropped her lipstick into her purse and let her purse slap close with a snap. She gave a quick rearranging twist to her shoulders and slipped her physics notebook into the crook of her arm. Everybody else was in class except for a couple of sophomores, who dashed into geography class and left Rhonda Fay Potts alone in the hall. She swung her purse by the handle and walked down the middle line.

I did not go to the prom. It had something to do with God, and I do not want to talk about it here. The morning after the prom, however, my cousin Sheryll called to tell me what it was like. She said it had been wonderful. The theme had been "In an Oriental Garden," and there had been a real full-sized teahouse with sliding freezer-paper doors. Sheryll said the juniors had covered the basketball timeclock with yellow crepe paper. She said it looked just like the moon.

Sheryll said, "You were the only person who wasn't there." I said, "I bet I wasn't the only person. Where could Katinka Freddleman get a date?"

Sheryll said, "Katinka Freddleman came with Miss Wompley. They sat around and drank punch and had matching corsages. Katinka sat around and acted like she was a teacher. She acted like she was somebody in charge. I told Mother I thought it was kind of gross. They were still there when Garvin Junior and I left."

I said, "Well then, what about Rhonda Fay Potts?" Sheryll said, "Rhonda Fay Potts was definitely there." Then she said, "Rhonda Fay Potts came on her own."

I said I didn't believe it, but Sheryll said, "Rhonda Fay Potts wore a formal and bought her own corsage and drove herself up to the door. She stayed a whole hour and got herself a cup of punch. She stood by herself the whole time."

I said, "Did anybody dance with her?" Sheryll waited a second; then she spoke very slowly so I could know that the words were all real. She said, "This is what you won't be believing. Rhonda Fay Potts danced by herself."

I said that couldn't have happened, but Sheryll said it was true. She said, "She stood around by herself and just moved around to the music. Then, when they played "Sherry, Baby," she came right out on the floor and did the Pony. The dress she had on was strapless. Everybody had to get out of her way. I told Garvin Junior it was time to go home."

Sheryll said it had been time to leave anyway, because there was a party at somebody's house. By the time they got there, two girls were already engaged, everybody was looking at rings, and the boys were trying to get drunk.

I asked her if it was much fun, but Sheryll said, "Not much fun—not really." She said everybody was weirded out about Katinka Freddleman and Miss Wompley. She said everybody kept talking about Rhonda Fay Potts out there under the time clock moon, by herself, dancing alone. She said it was the only thing anybody could remember at all.

Upstarts

Morning is not the only
good thing in the world

 HERE ARE, so I've heard, a great many things that can be accomplished before eight in the morning. If, however, those things cannot be accomplished while one is lying in bed — propped up on two pillows, eyes closed, shades drawn — as far as I am concerned, they can hold until noon.

I know lots of people who get things done in the morning. They get up at hours like six, five, and four-thirty. They talk a lot about crisp air, low cholesterol, and venture capital. They eat granola from a box and drink mugs of instant coffee which they refer to as "Java" and "Joe." They write Letters to the Editor. They find Willard Scott amusing.

They power-walk and "spend time with nature." If pressed, they can quote the poetry of James Whitcomb Riley. They probably order ceramic bird collections from the Franklin Mint.

They are not people whom I particularly enjoy. I figure they all sell Amway. I'll bet, deep down, a great many of them still believe the world is flat; I'll bet a lot of them honestly believe the lunar landings were filmed somewhere in Wyoming. They are people with far too much free time — and every one of them needs a nap by 3:45.

Worst of all, they feel they are somehow better than the rest of us. They feel they are somehow morally superior because they have made a successful trip to the bathroom before six A.M.

To them, the act of leaving one's bed in time to see the moon set is, in and of itself, an achievement worthy of universal admiration. They think it displays an enviable combination of back-slapping heartiness, gang-bustering initiative, and button-popping bonhomie. They feel they are a part of What Has Made This Nation Great. They are convinced that every day in their lives is a fifteen-minute episode of "Industry on Parade."

They think they know things the rest of us don't. All they really know is what time the garbage truck comes.

What dismays a slug-a-bed most about such people is their inordinately confrontational attitude toward even the most run-of-the-mill workaday morning. They order one another to get "up and at 'em." They "hit the floor running." They "seize" the day. They take the bull "by the horns." Images of flight and horror fill their lives.

I, on the other hand, have learned through years of experience, mornings, between the hours of five and six A.M., are perfectly content to be left alone. Never once can I remember a morning when I have felt the least compulsion to "rise," much less to "shine." I will, when forced, rise at 7:30, but I do not shine until three. Everything in between is negotiation.

The day and I begin by sizing each other up, jockeying for power, deciding who's-the-boss-here-anyway. Early risers assume that they must capitulate to morning simply because it is there. I do not. I prefer that a day present itself to me gradually, with an hour-or-so of soft music played on a grumbly clock radio that probably lost its sense of purpose sometime back around 1978. Then the power struggle begins.

If Tchaikovsky is being played, I chew on my pillow. If I hear Chopin, I roll over. A Richard Strauss tone poem lures one leg out from under the sheeting. The Pachelbel Canon sends it back again. If the Pachelbel is followed by a news bulletin or a report on the Zimbabwean army, all is lost. It is my responsibility to lie there and listen. I am not being lazy; I am being well informed.

It may take an organ toccata—or maybe an interview with Tommy Lasorda—but eventually the morning scores its first point in open competition. I am forced to get up and turn the radio off.

Then the pain hits.

I feel betrayed. I feel disoriented. I stand in the middle of the floor wearing a purple fraternity jersey that has lost its letters. I try to remember my name.

I only know I am glad I do not have a dog. If I had a dog, I would have to feed it. Right about now, it would need to go out.

A cup of coffee helps. It is instant, and I like it because it lets me stand and lean against the dishwasher while the water boils. If the coffee is too hot, I taste it and stir it very carefully. Then I drink every sip—sip after instant-coffee sip, standing there leaning against the dishwasher—before I even think about the shower.

In the shower I take a long time—even longer than I took with the coffee. In the shower I sing Gershwin and condition my hair. I make the morning suffer. I put it in its place. I face the world singing Gershwin, so that the morning will know who is in charge.

I did get up early one time. Now it seems a long time ago. I remember that I had to ride to East Tennessee in order to help three other people paddle a canoe down a river in the middle of a monsoon. We rode in someone else's car. Everybody else wanted to get an early start. I missed my coffee, and we saw the sun come up.

This is what it was like: The sky was all blackness, just like at night—except that now the blackness was growing softer, washing the color out of itself until it was light and blue. There still wasn't an actual sun, but the moon was already gone. There was just this one, glittery, flickering star, alone and fading in the pale soft sky.

There was no traffic on the interstate. Even opossums felt safe.

I thought if I didn't get some sleep I'd die. "So this is what morning's like," I said, trying to be a good participator.

"Just like this, once every twenty-four hours," said the driver, who had been up tying paddles on the roof of his Honda hatchback at four A.M. "Stay in bed, you miss this. Miss this, you miss the best part of the day."

"Uh-huh," I said, burying my face in a mildew-rotten life jacket.

I figured he didn't know there's another way to get at four A.M. It doesn't just begin the day; it also ends the night. If you just stay up long enough, it comes around that way too.

It looks, I promise you, very much the same from both ends. Either way, you get to see the garbage truck on Thursdays.

Prescription Only

Is Jell-O alive?

I DO NOT MIND going to the doctor. I am not afraid of anything a doctor may do to me. I am not afraid of anything that a doctor may say. I am not afraid of eight-foot-long stretches of black rubber tubing, nor am I afraid of where a doctor will think they should go.

I am, however, afraid of Jell-O. I am truly concerned that doctors, the persons entrusted with my health and personal well-being, think that it is something I should even occasionally eat.

I do not think doctors realize that Jell-O comes from an ill-defined food group. I do not think they understand that it can be yellow and green, both at once, and still taste like something that ought to be red. I do not think they realize that it is made from the ground-up hooves of cattle and horses and has a half-life of something like 852 years.

Doctors like to know that people out there awaiting bloodwork are subsisting on nothing more than Tropical Fantasy Jewel-Treat Fruit Jell-O. Doctors, who have not actually looked at a bowl of Jell-O since their third year of med school, consider it to be a part of a Clear Liquid Diet. I figure doctors have invested much of their disposable income in

Jell-O. I figure they are paying for sailboats with their dividend checks.

Doctors believe things they have heard from their mothers. They believe that Jell-O is somehow soothing and delightful and cool. They believe it has associations of tropical islands and palm trees and breezes blown from sapphire-blue seas. For most thinking adults who are not kept alive by IV-drip medication, however, Jell-O is generally associated with the night before the eight-foot-long black rubber tube. The prospect of the eight-foot rubber tube, meanwhile, pales in comparison to the prospect of an evening devoted to a tub of green Jell-O salad. For most procedures involving eight feet of black rubber tubing, you get to have Demerol. To face Jell-O, you have to stay wide awake and look at the bowl.

I figure most alert persons consider Jell-O to be somehow strangely disturbing. It is, after all, something made out of water, but it is also something you can chew. It is something you are supposed to eat while it is still wiggling. It is something that fights back when it is cut with a spoon. I am never precisely certain that it is not fully conscious of pain. I do not like to eat things that I fear are likely to scream. Among the peoples of certain primitive civilizations, I am sure it would be considered a work of the devil. Among paper-capped cafeteria workers standing behind sneeze-guards all across North America, however, it is considered dessert.

On the other hand, even cafeteria workers are not really quite sure. That is why they put little cups of green Jell-O at the beginning and at the end of the line. The Jell-O at the beginning of the line has carrots in it, while the Jell-O at the end of the line has grapes and a squirt of whipped cream. The carrots suggest that the Jell-O is a salad, but the grapes and the cream squirt define it as a luscious, albeit nonfilling, sweet treat. Many people going through cafeteria lines are eating lunch with their mothers. Sometimes, their mothers, who believe that a meal should have balance, get two servings of Jell-O at once. On the way home from the cafeteria, such mothers ask their children if Harry Truman is still President. In the emergency room, orderlies ask full-grown people if they have any idea why their mothers' tongues are lime green.

Mothers consider Jell-O to be a modern-age wonder. It is to the stomach what Mediterranean end tables are to interior design. It tastes best when it is served, during an "I Love Lucy" rerun, on a snap-together TV tray. Its flavors seem particularly vivid in a room where the carpet is shag. It can be molded and whipped and made foamy. It can be creamy-thick, or it can shimmer like glass. It can be used in recipes that call for nondairy whipped topping. It can give fruit cocktail a reason to be.

It can be bought in grocery stores in big plastic tubs which mothers save in a brown paper bag under the sink. People eat it and wonder whatever happened to the ozone. They eat it and forget just exactly why we got out of Vietnam. They begin to think good things about Richard Nixon. They begin to play albums by Steve Lawrence and Edie Gorme. They stay awake nights and try to remember the oldest Lennon Sister's name.

They trust that Jell-O is an American thing to believe in. They believe that it is, by definition, fine and good. They believe that it is nonfattening and refreshing and delightful. It reminds them of emeralds and rubies and shimmering hard-yellow diamonds. They put it on their cafeteria trays. They eat it because the doctor says so. They eat it with no questions asked.

They believe that it is precious and must be kept frozen. They do not realize that it could not, in any heat, in any way, ever be made to melt. They do not know that, merely because something is in the grocery freezer case, there is no guarantee that it actually needs to be cold. They do not know that sometimes things are merely created to look nice. They forget that some things are merely done as a ruse.

During the full four years of my college career, there was a cube of red Jell-O stuck to the dining hall ceiling. It had landed there during a food fight sometime in 1962, and it had been stuck to the crown molding ever since. The people in maintenance had figured it would stop being sticky one day and fall to the floor, but it did not. It just clung there on the crown molding and glistened in the electrically lit chandelier light.

For four years, it hung over our heads in the morning at breakfast; it hung there at lunchtime; it hung there at night. It stuck there and transformed itself into part of the building. It clung there and declined to dissolve. If I went back right now, it would probably be sticking there still—still shivering every time the air conditioning clicked on, still quivering every time some late-for-algebra sophomore slammed a dining hall door, still glittering with the just-add-water wonder of the American dream.

It is that cube I think of when I am forced to remember Jell-O. I would prefer to remember the tube.

Party Girl

The busiest woman in the world
writes her name nine thousand times

"And Jesus answered and said unto her,
Martha, Martha, thou art careful
and troubled about many things."
— Luke 10:41

MARTHA STEWART was maybe five minutes late for her book signing. For a lot of us, five minutes would not be much of anything; but I'll bet five minutes is a really big hunk of Martha Stewart's day. In five minutes, I figure, she could paint a house.

Fifteen minutes before Martha Stewart was even scheduled to show up and sign books with her on face on the cover, there were already maybe one hundred people in line. All of them were carrying very heavy Martha Stewart books, but no one of them was complaining. They knew full well that, however Martha Stewart was spending these five precious midafternoon minutes, she was spending them wisely. Whatever she was doing, she was not wasting time.

Everybody standing in line was white, except for one woman who was black. Everybody in line was a woman, except for three men, all of whom had brought cameras, so that they could take pictures of Martha Stewart signing their books. Nobody, not even the men with the cameras, grew one teeny-tiny bit testy. Instead, they spent their Martha-Stewart waiting time productively, in just the way Martha Stewart would spend her time if she ever had to wait for anything except a rented car.

Thrown together while waiting for Martha, two short women in pullover sweaters and turtlenecks confided to one another the problems they had both had at Christmas with their first croquemboches. "I never could get the glaze to set," one of them confessed in blank wonder. "I think the weather must have been wrong." The other woman asked her if she had carefully followed all of Martha's pictures. "Then," she said, "it must have been the damp."

Over the intercom, a voice from the front desk announced that Martha Stewart would soon be entering the building; all along the waiting line, feet began to shuffle and bodies began to stir. The speakers on the bookstore p.a. system began to play one of Martha's carefully prepared tapes of party music. Without the slightest announcement, the line had begun to move. Out of nowhere, Martha Stewart had materialized, tall and perfect and modestly winter-tanned and seated behind a table. Nobody had seen her come through a door.

Before anybody knew it, she was already signing books. Some people had brought a lot of Martha's books with them; some of them had *Martha Stewart Pies and Tarts* and *Martha Stewart Entertaining,* as well as *Martha Stewart Gardening,* which was supposedly the book Martha-Stewart people were buying on this particular day. Before Martha Stewart would sign any book, however, it had already been carefully opened to its title page. Whenever she looked down upon the title page before her, there was a yellow Post-It note, already clearly imprinted with the name she was expected to write. A bookstore employee was responsible for making sure the right names were on all the Post-It notes. Never once did Martha have to ask an embarrassing question. Never once did she have to ask twice how anything was spelled.

I asked a slender, blond, almost Martha-tall woman with a cordless telephone how many books Martha Stewart would sign while she was on a tour such as this. The blond woman had to pull out a pencil and add figures up. She said, "This is pretty amazing. This tour goes to twenty-eight cities. That means something like nine thousand books," she said. She stared at the paper; then she looked quickly at me. "Wow. Nine thousand books," she said. "Do you think there's any way I can be adding that right?"

At the signing table, a woman whose Post-It note had said "Cyndi" was taking Martha Stewart's picture. Martha sat with an already-signed book spread open before her. She smiled directly into the camera and held her signing pen in clear and open view, so that there was evidence that it was indeed her writing on the page. Cyndi, who was wearing a matching sweater-and-skirt set, said, "I wait for every one of your books. I love them. I buy them all." Martha's eyes were still healing up from the camera flash; but she smiled brightly in the direction of Cyndi's voice and said that was a nice thing to hear. "I know people ask you this a hundred times a day," Cyndi said, "but I have to know. How do you do it all?" Martha's pupils were getting smaller now. She smiled gently upon Cyndi and said, "I don't sleep."

Together, Cyndi and Martha Stewart had a little laugh. Then Martha handed Cyndi her just-signed book. Martha made sure not to close it so that the ink did not smear.

That morning, I had already heard Martha talk, during an interview on the radio, about never sleeping. During the same interview, she had also suggested that people (1) file all their seed packets in alphabetical order, (2) make their own pot-pourri, (3) encourage their children to grow okra, and (4) make sure to live in houses with screen windows so that they can hear the birds sing. Because I had planned to watch Martha Stewart sign books during the afternoon, I had called one of her people in New York to ask if it could be true that a woman somewhere in her early fifties could cook hundreds of plum puddings and never need sleep. With the frankness of a faith healer's assistant, a person fully accustomed to seeing the halt and the lame made miraculously whole, the woman on the telephone had said, "That's pretty much it."

In the bookstore that afternoon, Martha Stewart's time was almost up. She did not have to worry, however, because there were only three people left in line. She had almost made up her lost five minutes when her cordless-telephoned assistant stepped into the line. "Wait a minute, Martha," she said. "This is something you have to see."

She pushed forward a woman in a sweatshirt and windbreaker. In one hand the woman held a tiny copy of *Martha Stewart Entertaining,* smaller than a matchbook, just right for a dollhouse. At first, Martha Stewart did not know what she was seeing; then she asked the sweatshirted woman, "Where did this come from?" The woman in the sweatshirt said she had found the doll-size Martha-Stewart book in a store in New York. She seemed uncertain as to whether this was a good thing or not.

Martha told her blond assistant to be sure to get the New York store's address; then she whisked out her pen and scribbled something quickly on the tiny front page of the book. "Get your camera," she told her assistant, as she repositioned the book on her open palm. "Get in close," she said. "Be sure you get my hand."

After the Fact

Where are you, A. Edwin Fein, and why aren't you my father?

O N A VALENTINE'S Day evening, I read my mother's only
love letter. It was written to her in 1937 by a man named
A. Edwin Fein of 521 Fifth Avenue in New York City, New
York. Actually, "521 Fifth Avenue" was the address engraved
at the top of A. Edwin Fein's stationery. At the bottom of the
letter A. Edwin Fein had typed in his real address — way up on
the West Side, at 141st Street. I do not think that, in 1937, my
mother knew what it meant for a man to live that far up on the
West Side. I do not think she knew what it meant for his name
to be A. Edwin Fein.

Then again, I do not think A. Edwin Fein told much of the
truth about anything. I had read his love letter to my mother
many times before — it fell easily out of her college scrapbook
because she had never glued it in. Most of what was in her
scrapbook was candy wrappers and placecards, all of them
glued into the scrapbook so that they teetered at thrilling,
dramatic angles against the thick paper-felt blackness of the
wide-open page. All of the candy wrappers and placecards had
been carefully dated; their captions recorded precisely with
whom each candy bar had been eaten, next to whose placecard
each placecard had been found.

A. Edwin Fein's letter, however, had simply been stuffed in
between two black scrapbook pages — where it could be easily

found, or just as easily lost. Every time before when I had read it, I had never asked my mother if she and A. Edwin Fein had ever been in love. It was the only letter in her scrapbook from a man in New York City; the rest of the letters were from boys she had known in college. There was no letter from my father at all.

I had not read A. Edwin Fein's love letter in a long time. When I found it on this particular Valentine's Day evening, I must admit, it did not seem to be very much about love. Instead, it was mostly about somebody named Wilma. My mother had gone to a lot of trouble to find A. Edwin Fein's new address. She had apparently even had to contact this friend-in-common Wilma; it had taken my mother weeks and weeks to track down A. Edwin Fein.

I know it had taken weeks and weeks because the letter was written in mid-October, and the last time my mother had seen A. Edwin Fein was on a sunny afternoon outing to Jones Beach. Wilma had been there, and the three of them had gone to a concert. "After we parted that evening—I too did not realize it would be our last get together," A. Edwin Fein said in his errorlessly typed letter of precisely one page. "I mentioned to Wilma that I had forgotten to keep my promise to you."

When I read A. Edwin Fein's abandoned promise to my mother, this time as every time before, I found it hard to breathe. With only the caddishly clean-typed words that followed for evidence, I forced myself to piece together the events of that single shining day and evening at Jones Beach, that day when the vigilance of the fussy, intrusive Wilma must have made even the touch of a hand a furtive, impossible treasure. In the midst of that emotionally charged sunset, alas, while music drifted over the water from the Jones Beach floating stage, it seems that the only commitment A. Edwin Fein could manage was a promise to autograph my mother's Jones Beach concert program. As far as I know, this is the only promise the two of them ever shared.

Even though A. Edwin Fein never signed the program, my mother had offered to send him a cake. In his letter, A. Edwin Fein said that her offer was very generous but that, since it was not improbable that, by some remote chance, he might someday be in Alabama—where my mother had returned, long before she had been able to find A. Edwin Fein's true address—he might "someday" possibly avail himself of her "culinary accomplishments—IN PERSON," as he put it—all in majestic capital letters.

When A. Edwin Fein talked about Alabama, he called it "Alabamy," just like the Irving Berlin song about being "Alabamy-bound." He said that, in their brief, fleeting moments together, my mother had "radiated" the thrill of seeing New York for the first time. Adding something about "the genuineness of people's feeling and appreciation," A. Edwin Fein said he hoped my mother—who had gone to New York, of all things, to attempt a career on the stage—had "derived much of practical benefit" from her time there. A. Edwin Fein signed his letter with a one-word "Sincerely." He did not say, "Sincerely yours"; there was no mention of a plighted troth. He added, in a P.S., that Wilma's mother's health had improved.

My mother had once told me she had almost married a rich man. One day, while I was sitting in the kitchen watching her can quart jars of little pearl-gray-colored field peas, I asked her if that rich man had been somebody called A. Edwin Fein. My mother turned the heat down under the kettle she was using to blanch the field peas. She said, "Wherever did you come up with A. Edwin Fein's name?" I told her she had saved his letter in her college scrapbook; I told her he had written to her from New York, on stationery that had been engraved.

My mother poured the freshly washed field peas into the barely boiling water, which splashed out and made little steam spots on the top of the stove. She said A. Edwin Fein was not anyone she had ever intended to marry. The only rich man she had ever thought of marrying, she said, was somebody from Texas; his family had something to do with oil.

In the back of my mother's college scrapbook, far away from A. Edwin Fein's letter, there is a newspaper clipping, announcing plans for a recital in which my mother was to give dramatic readings, spelled every so often by a girl who played Fritz Kreisler tunes on the violin. The announcement said that my mother's major contribution to the evening would be a recitation of scenes from the novel *If I Were King*. The announcement said, with surety, that my mother had plans to "make a profession of her art."

The announcement appeared in my mother's hometown paper in 1928. It was years before she ever went to New York, just as it was years before she received her letter from A. Edwin Fein. One day, while she was blanching field peas, I asked her to recite her scenes from *If I Were King*, but she said she could not remember even how to begin. When I asked her to tell me about the concert at Jones Beach, she said she could not remember any of the music she had heard.

The Bread of Wisdom

I'm a *goy* — what
the hell do *I* know?

I AM NOT SURE how bagels became central to my life. I have not known them since birth; they are most certainly not something my mother knew how to cook. They are not even something my mother knew how to buy, mostly because bagels are something she was never given a chance to learn.

Never once in her life — which was, by any standard, of at least a moderate length — did she enter a store where a bagel was buyable. She did not frequent establishments with gourmet counters. Grocery stores in communities with 94 percent Baptist populations were not in need of a kosher shelf. Only once did my father attempt to introduce her to a sandwich from a delicatessen. It was made with rye bread and sauerkraut, and she said it made her burp. She could not comprehend any ethnic food that did not require a can on the back of the stove for the collection of grease. She had never even seen an Episcopalian, much less a Jew; there was no way she was going to accept the concept of boiling dough.

I do not, of course, feel particularly alone in any of this. I am not sure there is, anywhere out there, proof of the existence of bagels anywhere before 1975. I do not find record of them anywhere in literature. Photographic evidence is disturbingly scant. In the few bagel-antiquity-supportive photographs that I have examined, I find suggestions of the skillful, if subtle, retouch. As far as I know, I was there when they began to exist.

A boy named Wayne bought me my first bagel on a New York street corner somewhere on the East Side, way up in the sixties. It cannot have been one minute earlier than 1978. I know, because I was wearing a trench coat with a lining that had to be zipped in. Wayne, who was from Fayetteville, Georgia, was looking for Persian cigarettes. He said that, whenever he came to Manhattan, he picked up Persian cigarettes by the case. On this particular day, he found them at a newsstand, a door or so off Lexington, but, because they cost $8.97, he only bought one pack. Wayne said, "I've never heard of such a thing," and flipped up the sheared fake-fur collar on his black-and-white tweed coat. He said, "Let's go eat something," and let the door slam behind us as he pulled me out to the street.

On the corner there was a guy selling hot dogs and pretzels that smelled like the dirty New York November air. Wayne lit a thirty-five-cent cigarette and said, "Thank God. I'm dead for a bagel." He said, "Don't worry, I'm buying." He rummaged around on the hot dog-and-pretzel guy's pushcart counter. He slapped mustard on a barely beige bathtub-stopper-sized bagel. He held it out to me in a piece of waxed paper. He lipped his crackling extravagant cigarette and said, "Eat this. It's just a bagel, but it may have to be your whole lunch." The bagel cost less than Wayne's cigarette. As far as I know, he had invented them both on that day, on the spot.

Wayne blotted his mouth with his waxed paper napkin and said, "Couldn't you just live on bagels—that is, of course, if you could get them anywhere outside the civilized world?" I said, "God yes, I love them." Standing there on a street corner, with the gray sky spitting down sleetdrops, I convinced myself I had heard the word "bagel" somewhere before. I had already done the same thing with "Aquascutum" and "Sulka." I bit into my bagel and took a waxed-paper swipe at my mouth. Wayne started a catty-cornered jaywalk across the intersection. He said he had to go on to Hermés.

I chewed clumsily along on my bagel, which sprung gloomily back when I bit it. It was like eating a dog's rubber toy. I was not sure if this was supposed to be a good bagel. I am not sure I know to this day. I have learned that each bagel, like each person who eats it, lives by its own set of values. It cannot, and will not, be judged. It neither accepts nor acknowledges a jury of peers.

I came to the bagel late, without standards. I knew it could not be exotic, since it was nothing more than not-quite-brown bread. I merely knew it was something vaguely redolent of all things impressively urban. It could not be created, I knew, without mammoth industrial ovens. Any city that could boast of bagels was alert and all-knowing. In such a city lived people who drove perfectly maintained two-decade-old silver Jaguars, people who bought paintings that did not look like jugs full of flowers, people who had the *Times* delivered to their doors every day. People who ate bagels, I knew without anyone saying it, were people who could name every member of the President's cabinet. They were people for whom cleverness did not mean a thing.

Then, on a Saturday afternoon, I found bagels on a shelf at the grocery store. They had arrived in the Age of the New Awareness of Bread. They were stocked, not in gourmet foods or kosher foods or ethnic foods, but in "Specialties." They were lined up alongside baguettes and Italian rolls and sourdough buns from San Francisco. They were there where anyone could have them. They were packed in plastic bags, portioned out in different flavors—some with raisins, some with oat bran—all of them ready for the freezer, all of them bereft of chemical preservatives and high in complex carbs. Each package of bagels contained a half dozen, right for breakfast for a family of four. People strolled by and dropped them in shopping carts, next to their magazine-rack copies of *Town and Country* and the *Times*.

These are the bagels I buy now, and I buy them often. I take them home and slice and toast them and eat them late at night like cupcakes, except for the jar of grainy mustard on the side. They are bland and crisp against the burn of ice-cold vodka. In the morning, they are crisp and sharp against apple juice.

My friend Berneice, who runs an art gallery somewhere in Soho, says I have no idea how bagels should be. She says I am content with my plastic-bagged bagels because I am completely and entirely a *goy*. From New York now she sends me bags full of bagels. They are hard, garlicky little knots of dough that must be torn fiercely apart with the teeth. Berneice says I must never toast them. She says toasting bagels is a very *goy* thing to do.

I let Berneice's bagels sit in their brown paper bag in the refrigerator, where they dry into mean little fists. They grow so hard that they cannot be chewed. I wait them out, and then I eat my off-the-shelf bagels. I toast them until they are totally devoid of context. At no moment do they remind me of anywhere I have ever been.

Sabrina Fair

She was Audrey Hepburn; she made grown men weep

G OD DID NOT make Audrey Hepburn for the fantasies of little boys. For that use, God made the likes of Rita Hayworth and Lana Turner, women drawn with a couple of wide-swirling strokes of a blood-red lipstick, hastily sketched in with a sure, practiced hand—womanhood reduced and stylized and then idealized into a double-handful of curves, easy to remember—women about whom stories did not have to be made up.

Audrey, however, was drawn in detail. Nothing about her beauty seemed sure or uncomplicated. Everything about her was intricate filigree. In a self-congratulatory, over-uphol-stered post-war world, she was frail. Sometimes, when she was not wearing dinner-length gloves, her elbows could jut out at an ungainly angle. Whenever she pulled her hair back, her ears looked all wrong.

In recompense, nevertheless, there was a long, slender nose between a pair of immaculately hollow cheekbones. There were her huge doelike, innocent, world-weary eyes that never went blank, eyes that winced under every blow, eyes that never missed the punchline of a joke, eyes that questioned every lover's glance. There was her waist, tiny enough to be clutched in the grasp of a single palm. There was the simple, immaculate arch of her neck, so poignant it could reduce grown men to tears.

When teen-age girls saw her in her bare-shouldered ballgown in *Sabrina*, they looked down at their own Ava Gardner-inspired bosoms and felt sorely ashamed. When she stood on Fifth Avenue, leaned back into an immaculate French curve, and looked into a window at Tiffany's, Weight Watchers and the entire aerobics industry were born.

It was not easy for little boys to comprehend such a curious kind of beauty. If they touched her, they feared she would break. It took older men like Bogart in *Sabrina*, Cary Grant in *Charade*, or Astaire in *Funny Face* to handle her gently and keep their own hearts at a distance. They could tell, mostly by the deep, soughing hush of her voice, that she was fully capable of disturbing their souls. Although they were men of experience, she was not exactly like any girl they had ever seen before in their lives; but, because they were men of experience, they found in her the precise memory of every girl they had ever loved.

Because Audrey was flat-chested and because she was barely nineteen, Hollywood tried as hard as it could to transform her into Debbie Reynolds playing the Blessed Virgin Mary, but, completely without premeditation or the slightest trace of ill spirit, she kept coming out as Salome. She was Melisande and Catherine Earnshaw and the somehow-escaped Anastasia. She was moth, but she also was flame.

That must be what the powdery old Colette saw when, as legend has it, she got her first glimpse of Miss Audrey Hepburn, B-movie bit-player, in a Monte Carlo hotel lobby and decreed her to be the only girl with any right to play her Gigi on the stage. Again and again, in *Roman Holiday* and *Sabrina* and *My Fair Lady* and *Funny Face* and *Breakfast at Tiffany's*, Audrey would play this same role—a princess striving in vain to pass for a commoner, a sterling teaspoon merely waiting to be polished, a foundling adrift in the wrong world.

Certainly, no matter how many times unthinking people say otherwise, what Colette saw in Audrey Hepburn—and what, in memory, makes grown men weep—had nothing to do with "gamine charm." Never once was she any good at playing a guttersnipe, which is why at least the first half of her Eliza Dolittle is ill fitted and wrong. She was not born to the streets; her mother was a baroness. The way she glided across an outdoor dance floor with Gregory Peck or the way she floated lightly down a staircase in a burst of flashbulbs and red Givenchy chiffon was not anything that could in any way be taught.

Even the hunger and ugliness of World War II Holland had their part in her fairy tale; she had, like all certifiable princesses, spent her time in the witch's tower; she had survived her time in the ogre's cave. She would not forget their horrors, but she would escape them. In the movies, she would convince the rest of us, sometimes even for a stretch of two full hours, that it might have been nothing more than a miserable, unconscionable dream. But behind her eyes there was always the trouble. Whenever she touched the meatless arm of a child in Somalia, the pain must have always returned.

What remains most vividly of Audrey Hepburn is that moment when most of us saw her for the first time—as the Princess Ann, waving to her public in the disturbingly believable "documentary" footage of *Roman Holiday*. The way we remember her voice—its strange, Continental, not-quite-identifiable accent, its slight, squeaky edge under stress—is with her first words, "I hate my nightgown. I hate *all* my nightgowns. And I hate my underwear too!" The year was 1953, and, even though we never learned the name of her country, we knew she was a princess. She might have her one day of freedom and smoke her first cigarette and dance on a barge with Gregory Peck; but we knew that, at midnight, like some turned-about Cinderella, she would return to her job. The palace gates would open, and she would slip magically in.

The next morning, in a hall filled with reporters, she would face the man who had given her her first kiss. Her eyes would glisten, but she would not break down. She would touch his hand, and they would part forever. Because he was a reporter, he would head off to file his story; because she was a princess, she would return to the throne of the unnamed country to which she was born.

She would be wearing white gloves and a huge skirt made of yards of organdy. When she left the hall, she would hold her head high, and the curve of her neck would be achingly sweet. In 1953, this is how princesses acted; even now, and even in memory, Audrey still puts the real thing to shame.

Southern Comfort

If it weren't for a pitcher of iced tea, we probably wouldn't have Atlanta

 A SOUTHERN MAN always orders iced tea. That is how you know he is Southern. He orders it in places like the Oak Bar of the Plaza and does not feel the least bit odd. Even when he asks the bartender—who is running the blender at "frappe" for a couple of hookers who are sitting at the corner so they can watch the room—if he could maybe get some Sweet 'n' Low, he still does not feel strange.

The bartender looks at him over a pair of peach daiquiris as if he had just been handed a tract by a Jehovah's Witness and says, "Sure, fella, and while we're at it, why don't I start ya a tab?" Across the bar, the man wrinkles his tanned-skin brow for a moment and then says, "Yeah, maybe I should run a tab. I may be having more tea."

This does not mean this man is stupid. It does, on the other hand, mean he is Southern. It means he has a cousin named Jimmie who is a girl and a cousin named Melvin Jr. who is not quite right. It means that he still checks restaurant menus to see if they offer fried okra. It means that, when he takes over small corporations, he does it in a pair of Bass Weejuns and a button-down-collar shirt.

None of this is the Southern guy's fault. Most of it is the fault of his father, who did not serve as a strong enough role model during those important formative years of three to eight, and his mother, who let him roll out the biscuits.

Now he drinks iced tea as an involuntary reaction. He does it without thinking, in the same way he shakes his legs when he stands up in his boxer shorts. Iced tea flows down in his veins from his mother — the same way the crotch-drop instinct comes down to him from his dad.

Together, the three of them — in the kitchen or around the dining room table with a cloth spread for company — drank iced tea every day. They drank it after cocktails, and they drank it before. Nobody asked whence it came. It had no vintage year. It forced no decision except "Sweet or Unsweet?" It simply was.

It was like the set of teak-handled steak knives and the little pink plastic latticework holder stuffed with bifolded white paper napkins with a blue-daisy trim. It was there. Nobody dared ask the question, Who Made It? It was there, close to the freezer on the top shelf of the refrigerator. It was simply there. It was like cornbread. It was like God.

People from other places — places like the Oak Bar of The Plaza on a Friday afternoon — do not understand about iced tea. They do not understand about its impact on the economy: They do not understand that it is the reason people in places like Mississippi — people who have been crunching shoe-sized ice chunks with their bare teeth three times daily since 1947 — now have mouths full of fillings while their dentists have houseboats and summertime vacation homes.

Neither do they comprehend its importance to the culture of our nation at large: They do not understand that the true source of the Southern gift to talk and tell stories is a build-up of residual caffeine. They think most of the South has been asleep since 1902. The truth is that, for something like the last nine decades, most of southern Georgia has been buzzed out of its mind.

People from other places feel that an iced-tea order — particularly in any month ending with an *R* — suggests a naive and uncalculating mind. They make the Southern guy drink it out of a glass that was designed to hold Really Sophisticated Things — things like whiskey sours, sloe gin fizzes, and Bongo Barracuda Blinders. The Southern guy, however, is not embarrassed. He figures this is the only glass the bartender can find.

The bartender has, in fact, never served a glass of iced tea before in his life. He has to brew it from two old bags of Soochong Oolong Grey that he found in a drawer next to the multicolored cocktail-olive-pick swords. He has no earthly idea what to charge.

But the Southern guy doesn't care. It is Friday afternoon. He has left his Weejuns somewhere upstairs.

He is now sitting on a bar stool in this very expensive hotel, wearing an $875 Italian silk suit and a $900 pair of Italian low-vamp loafers, and he is stirring this glass of iced tea with a little red-and-white peppermint-striped all-purpose swizzle stick/straw. He is happy as two hushed puppies. The hookers look at him like they expect him to start either passing out his Jehovah's Witnesses pamphlets or trying to sell them whole-life insurance.

The Southern guy, meanwhile, sips his whiskey-sour glass of iced tea and thinks he is living a normal life. This is because he is Southern. It is the only life he knows.

There is no morality involved. It is a natural reaction, a decision above right and wrong. It does not mean much of damn anything. It does not mean he likes the way this iced tea — or any iced tea — tastes. It does not mean he will not be having a double Dewar's-and-water in something like a minute-and-a-half. It does not mean the hookers need to be worried in the least.

What it does mean is that, even if he is not hot now, this guy has been hot before. He has sipped on iced tea — strong-brewed from hot water, not made from an odd-foamy cold-water mix — and survived.

He has held the ice in his jaw on soggy-cotton-aired days and felt the side of his face grow numb from the freeze. He has sucked long slurps of tea through a straw on still, bug-drowsy afternoons and heard people tell tales. He has known nights when the clink of the iced-teaspoon handles was the only thing keeping the air alive. He has seen people drop dead with a glass of iced tea in their hands. He has seen women give birth with a glass of iced tea by the bed.

If he does not drink it now, he will be somehow disloyal. He will go back to his room and discover his boxers have all turned to briefs. He will not know exactly who he is, but he will know he is not exactly himself.

He does not care what a bartender and a couple of hookers with on-the-house daiquiris think. He knows, at this moment, who he is. He is a man with signing privileges at this hotel. He is a man whose Weejuns are outside his room door waiting to be shined. He is a man who knows his own rules:

It is too late in the day for a Dr. Pepper. He is having iced tea.

Talk Is Cheap

It's 6:30—do you really
want to pick up the phone?

I AM HAVING A relationship with a woman. Her name is Gloria, and she wants to shampoo my rugs. She told me so the very first time we met.

We met on a Tuesday night at 6:30. I know it was a Tuesday night because I was having two toasted bagels, some grapes, and a tub of cottage cheese. On those nights I try not to eat fat because on Tuesday night I do not go to the gym. On Tuesday nights I eat bagels and watch TV shows. That's how I know it was a Tuesday; I was leaning against my refrigerator, watching the old bagel crumbs catch fire in the toaster when I heard the telephone ring.

She said, "Hi, is this John? This is Gloria. I'm calling from California." Her voice was slightly throaty—a little husky but not in any way mannish. There was something about it that said she was smoking a cigarette. Generally, I am not attracted to smokers. But I knew right away Gloria was different. There was a soft, smooth hotness to the way she said my name.

I said, "Gloria, what are *you* doing in California?" I thought, "California is a long way away."

Gloria said, "I'm in California because I live here." The nonfiltered smoke ring of her voice curled up into an ungiddy swirl of pack-a-day laughter. She said, "Right now, out here in California, I'm talking to you."

I thought, "This must be costing Gloria a lot of money." I said, "Gloria, do I know who you are?"

In the distance I thought I heard the sharp fizzling crack of a paper match bursting to hot-open flame. I heard Gloria inhale slowly as she eased the crisp smoke deeply down and in. She said, "No, John, I really don't think so." She said, "Do you have hardwood floors, or do you have rugs?"

I thought, "Gloria is probably going to be reimbursed for this call." I said, "Gloria, I'm sorry but you've caught me at dinner. I'm getting ready to eat cottage cheese."

Gloria said, "I know, John. I called now because I thought I might catch you. That's the way I work." She paused a second. I thought I heard a fast little rush of hot breathed-out smoke. She said, "Now, tell me about your carpets. Do you feel that you're getting them clean?"

I said, "I don't clean my carpets. I vacuum them every six months, on a Saturday, right after I've scrubbed the tub." I said, "I'm sorry, Gloria, but my bagels are ready. I don't think I want to talk about this now."

I could hear Gloria leaning, urgent and tight, into the receiver. She said, "Oh, John, don't you know unshampooed carpets are alive with tiny microorganisms? There are invisible little living things right now in your carpet—things that breed in the fibers and spread filth and disease."

I said, "Gloria, I'm eating my dinner. I know how micro-organisms work."

Gloria said, "John, I'm calling you with a wonderful oppor-tunity. I could arrange an appointment for you. There would be no obligation at all. I don't know you, but what I'm saying to you possibly could even save your life." Her words now were tumbling forward in a close, husky whisper, as if she were making a dope deal, as if her husband were listening from around the corner, from the very next room, through a door she had closed but not locked. She was rushing through her words as if she had to speak quickly, as if she were being watched. I could tell she had stubbed out her cigarette now; I could see her pounding it frantically into a thick restaurant-issue ashtray. It broke into a crooked little angle as she ground it hard into the ashtray with her sharp-perfect purple-red nails.

I said, "Gloria, I'm not ready for this kind of commitment."

She said, "Don't worry. If it doesn't work out, I won't call again."

I said, "Gloria, that's not what I want."

She said, "I know, John. That's how it has to be." Gloria did call again. She called the next Tuesday, while I was waiting for my microwave potato to bake. This time she didn't even say my name; she did not have to say hers. There was no hello and no small talk. There was just a heavy-aired "How did it go?"

I was fumbling in my knife drawer to find a still-working corkscrew. I said, "Gloria, you said you wouldn't call back."

She said, "I'm just checking to see how things went. It's no big deal. It's just something I do once in a while—" For no reason that had any logic, her sentence came still to a pause. Then she said, "—for people, for people who've seemed sort of nice."

I said, "Gloria, I don't know what to say."

She said, "Do you want to use Mastercard or set up your own payment plan?"

I said, "Gloria, I just cannot do this."

She said, "Was it the appointment? Was it something the floor-covering sanitation analysis representative said?" For the first time since I had known her, Gloria's voice was rising higher. I heard it growing frantic and panicked and thin. She said, "I'm out here in California. There's only so much I can do."

I wedged the phone receiver between my ear and my shoulder while I opened my just-home-from-the-store bottle of wine. Sometimes I drink wine on Tuesdays because wine has absolutely no fat grams at all. I said, "Gloria, let's not let this get ugly."

Gloria had her words back under control now. She spoke slowly, and there was almost no trembling at all. She said,

"Look, I'm going to leave you my 800 number. If you want me, you know where I'll be."

I put down my wine glass — I figured I owed her that much. I said, "Gloria, you live in California. California is a long way away." Out in California, Gloria eased the receiver down slowly. She did not slam it. The air simply passed into a long hapless drone.

A couple of Sundays later I talked to my father. The first thing he asked was, "How's Gloria been?" My father has moments of bright shining hope.

I said, "Gloria and I don't talk much these days."

My father said, "I suppose this had something to do with your rugs." It was as if he had caught me wearing lingerie. He said, "Your mother and I knew this was how it would be."

The next Tuesday I waited by the phone until 6:30 while my salmon steak was getting charred on the grill. I let the phone ring twice before I picked it up. The voice on the line said, "Hi, John, this is Stephanie. I'm calling from Minneapolis-St. Paul."

I said, "Wow, Stephanie, it must really be nice there." Stephanie said, "Actually, we've been having some rain."

She said, "I hope I'm not disturbing your evening, but you may be spending too much on your home equity loan."

I said, "Frankly, I didn't have plans for the evening. I was just going to watch some TV." Outside on the grill, my salmon steak was a black wedge of ashes. Somewhere up in Minneapolis, Stephanie was striking a match.

Closet Drama

At the end of summer,
there are gentle ways of saying good-bye

 O N AN EARLY autumn morning not that long ago, all alone and by myself, I did an awful thing: I lied to my summer blazer. I put my summer blazer back in the closet and told it a bold-faced lie. I told my summer blazer it could hang there all winter, between the pink linen jacket and the white flannel trousers with the pleated front, and I would take it out again in the spring — maybe at Easter, when I would wear it with a boater and a sharp new regimental tie, crisply tied and dimple-knotted at the neck.

I promised we would go on picnics and to dinner on a lake in Northern Michigan. I said we would go back to London and watch the flowers making madness again in St. James's Park. I promised we would linger over champagne on long, simple Sunday afternoons that drifted softly into dusk.

But I lied.

My summer blazer is nine years old. It has shiny spots on both shoulders, two button holes are frayed, and the lining hangs down and catches things in the back. When I button it, I cannot breathe. It will not see another summer. It will not have another spring.

I could have been a man and told the truth. Blazers have no ego. They do not make a scene.

Blazers know they are replaceable, in a way that pink linen jackets and lime-green pants embroidered with palm trees do not. They do not make fashion statements.

Each one is navy blue. Each one has three front buttons embossed with large dead sheep. Each one has patch pockets and a single vent in the back. They are all made of hopsacking. They are not cute in any way.

And they are never, never on sale. If they are on sale, they are not blazers. If they are on sale, they are — at closer inspection — something else. Something with deep-wine top stitching and leatherette trim on the lapels. Something that women buy for their husbands. Something that comes with a matching tie-and-pocket-handkerchief set. Something people wear home on their first day out after serving seventeen-and-a-half years in the state penitentiary for passing hot checks. Something that means to make trouble.

The blazer, however, does its best not to be difficult. It does not require one to have a highly developed sense of color and pattern at 6:45 on a Tuesday morning. Other things do not have to worry about matching the blazer. It is the blazer's job to match anything involving any of the three primary colors — and not to act uppity in the process.

If it doesn't get stained in the grass, looks Pretty Damn Sharp With a Pair of Chinos, and can still be buttoned, at least while you're standing up, the blazer gets to hang around for about nine years. And then it is gone.

On a mid-September Saturday, it gets slipped to the back of the closet next to another blazer, the one you bought in 1972 for a job interview with an ad agency in Toledo, Ohio. The idea is that, one day, you will try them on again, and they will fit. The idea is that, on Friday nights, you will wear them with jeans. The truth is, You Won't.

But you do not throw them away. If you threw them away,

you would look down the next morning and start finding hair in the drain. The hair would be your own.

In a week, the doctor would suggest you try a fiber supplement. By the end of October, you would be watching fishing programs on public television. Then, one day—maybe in as little as six months, you would actually dial an 800 number and order a gold velour lounge chair. You would starting letting Ed McMahon advise you on the planning of your estate.

Apparently, women do not understand clothing in this way. Apparently, melancholy does not touch their lives. They do not save their first pair of five-inch heels or their first padded bra. Women have yard sales, and life goes on. They do not feel the ache of transition.

In a woman's life, abruptness is all: On August 31 she can wear white patent-leather stilettos and be taken seriously. On September 2 she can't. Fussiness is not required. If she bucks the natural order, she pays the price: People mistake her for Bella Abzug and she wishes she had never been born. It is a beautifully balanced system—exquisite as algebra.

For a man in September, meanwhile, every day is a moral mine field. He runs his fingertips along the fraying sleeve hem of his blue hopsacking blazer and ponders his mortality.

He knows this blazer well. It is a blazer to be trusted. Breezes seek it out. So does the shade of large trees. So do people in white coats with silver trays full of gin-and-tonics in glasses so frosty they burn the hand. If he puts this blazer away, he may never know these things again.

To put this blazer away is to say that something is done—something more than summer. It is to admit that September is the meanest of months, the month in which men grow old. That is why, on a mid-September Saturday, I lied to my summer blazer.

I do not think women understand this sort of thing.

Track Record

The *Hummingbird* flew by at sunset; it did not slow down

F ROM OUR FRONT porch, just at sunset, we could see the lights of the dining-car windows fly past. I am certain all the trains had names, but this one was called the *Hummingbird*. As far as I can remember, it is the only train name I ever really knew.

We would wait for it every night — my mother, my brother, and I — sitting on the porch and telling long, made-up stories. In the distance, on the right evenings, the *Hummingbird*'s whistle would be high and steady and sweet; its rumble would be gentle and constant and low. It did not slow for anything; there was no reason for it to pause anywhere in the night. Instead, it hurtled past, the slippery, orange-purple sunlight dancing across its sleek, blood-red skin as the *Hummingbird* slid away into the night.

The railroad tracks were maybe 150 yards from our front porch. On evenings before summer had set in, we could see the low, shaded lamps on the dining-car tables. We could see the yellow glow they dribbled out into the long, pale-colored room. In the windows, men in gray suits and white-gloved women leaned toward each other over stiff cardboard menus. Black men in white jackets moved through the dining car with pots of coffee and glass pitchers of iced water and tea.

My mother would tell us about the times she had taken the train to New York City and Chicago and about the way the even, purring rumble of the tracks had lulled her to sleep. In the night, she said, the Pullman cars were drowsy and silent. When she lifted the little curtains that covered her windows, she said, she could see the moonlight flying across the dark shapes of trees.

It would take only this tiny bit of a story, and then the *Hummingbird* would be gone, its wheels making a few quiet, clicking sounds on the train tracks, its whistle singing high and unbroken and beautiful into the night. My mother would lean forward in her porch chair and listen for the last bit of sound to fade away. "You never know who might be on that train any night while we're watching," she would say. "It could be somebody important. It could be Howard Keel and Kathryn Grayson. They could be sitting there having their supper on their way out to Hollywood. You never know where people are headed. They could be there, but you just never know."

Without saying anything, we would sit very still and watch the car lights traveling down the highway alongside the train tracks. Then, out of nowhere, my brother would jump down out of the porch swing and ask, "When people on a train have to go to the bathroom, what do they do?"

My mother would stand up and say she figured it was time for our supper. By the time she could get it on the table, she would say, our father would probably be home.

The train we took was not the *Hummingbird*. Instead, in the middle of a Friday afternoon, while the sun was still high, my mother buttoned me and my brother into our matching sports coats and held each of us still while she slicked down our cowlick-mad hair. We were going to have our train experience, she said, even if it could not be the *Hummingbird*. She said we would have to take the early train if we were going to reach Montgomery in time for supper. "Hold onto my hands. We'll meet your daddy when we get to the station," she said.

While she pulled our stiff cloth caps down hard on our foreheads, she explained that, on the nights when we saw the *Hummingbird*, it was fighting hard as it could to get to the end of Alabama. Even if we could make it stop for us, she said, it would not be headed for Montgomery at all. My mother locked the front-porch door. With my brother and me each holding one of her white-gloved hands, we walked to the train depot.

Before we were halfway down the driveway, my brother announced that he was going to have ice cream in the dining car. My mother, however, told him we would eat when we got to Montgomery. She said we would meet my father and eat in a restaurant and go to a movie. She said the kind of train we were taking probably did not even have a dining car. After we had finished our movie, she said, our father would drive us home.

The train that stopped for us was a dust-pallid green. When it slowed itself down for the depot, its brakes made a tight wheezing sound. A lone black man in a dusty blue uniform stepped heavily down into the gravel, placed a wooden-box step in front of my mother, and slowly lifted my brother and me up into the train.

On the train car, most of the seats were empty. A man in a short-sleeved white shirt was reading a Bible. A man in overalls stretched his legs out over a couple of armrests and went directly to sleep. My brother and I sat on either side of my mother and, once in a while, glanced out the window. Outside, the blank fields and the pine trees tumbled past us wildly in the early spring sunlight. The railroad tracks clung hard to the edge of the highway. Everything that blurred past us was something we already knew.

My brother slipped down from his seat and walked slowly back and forth in the aisle, climbing up into empty seats, leaning against windowsills, and staring at the countryside flying dryly past on either side of the car. The man in the white shirt looked at my brother for a second and then went back to reading his Bible. My brother tiptoed carefully past the man in the overalls. The sleeping man stretched his legs and made a dull snoring sound.

The black man in the dusty blue uniform passed through the car, this time carrying an armful of bags of boiled peanuts. I looked up at my mother, and she handed me a nickel. She let me buy the bag of peanuts; then she took it quietly from me and slipped it into her purse. "If we eat them now," she said, "they'll spoil our supper." She said we would save the peanuts for later. We would eat them together in the movie theater, when nobody was watching. We would share them, she said, when it was dark, sitting together and passing the bag among us, watching the flashing light on the screen.

Shameless

Coming to an understanding
with Garth Brooks's rear end

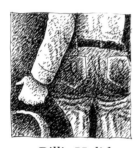

I'M NOT SURE I like myself very much anymore. I've been listening to Garth Brooks. I have been singing along.

This was not supposed to happen to me. I was not supposed to be having fun. I was supposed to be listening to Billie Holiday. I was supposed to be into the way Billie Holiday could turn even "Jeepers, Creepers" into a convincing argument for drug education in our schools. Or I was supposed to be into Maria Callas with her raw-throated, unhealable voice that always reminded me of a nightmare I had in the eighth grade. It was a nightmare about being naked in band practice and having to stand up and play a flute solo and not having much of a tanline and not knowing what to do with my hands.

I was supposed to be into dead women who had had really rotten relationships with men. I was supposed, maybe, to be into Patsy Cline—or Loretta, who, even though she is still alive, can have some really bad days. I was not supposed to be into Garth Brooks.

I am not listening to Garth Brooks, mind you, because I think he feels much about anything. What I like is the warbly sort of yodely sound he makes on everything. It is the same sound he makes when he is singing about wife abuse or when he is singing about riding a bull. It is not the sound of a guy who is very worried about being left lonely or never finding a job. It is not the sound of a guy who wakes up any morning feeling a little confused to be greeted by wallpaper he has never seen before. It is not the sound of a guy who gets nervous and doesn't make the one phone call he wants to make until it is too late to call anybody on Friday night. It is merely the sound of a guy who likes making sounds, a guy who can get drunk without hangovers and become amazingly rich simply by singing about what gee-willy-damn fun it is to pull stupid-man-fool tricks if you claim they were tricks pulled for love.

It is the sound of sheer male looney-tooney bravado, not the silk-shirt-over-smooth-pecs, gentle-handed, slow-dancing, high-minded Ricky Van Shelton baritone or the damned-if-I'll-be-pussy-whipped-again nose whine of George Strait, or the good-guys-don't-have-hormones, tight-jeans tenorino of Clint Black. It is the post-Mandrell, here-we-are-in-the-'90s idea of how country music should sound.

It does not matter if Garth Brooks actually sounds as if he has ever been to a rodeo. Nobody hearing him has ever been to a rodeo either. It does not matter if he actually sounds like a wife beater. It is not as if wife beaters across America might flock to reveal themselves after the experience of having heard Garth Brooks sing. It does not matter if he actually sounds like a good-old-boy at a champagne reception. Nobody pretends anymore that these are songs about hard-drinking honky-tonk reality. They are songs about country music, which makes them games that are fun to play. That is why Garth Brooks finds them fun to sing. That is why, I think, I like to sing them too.

They are not about anything I know about. They are not about the sort of codependent, obsessive-compulsive behavior I keep tripping up on in a song by Rodgers & Hart or Cole Porter. Merely thinking about a Lorenz Hart lyric can make me uneasy. I can sing along with Garth Brooks, however, and be really-truly unfeignedly happy because not much of what he says—given my Japanese-car-driving, yes-I-will-have-a-martini life—makes very much sense.

What does make sense, meanwhile, is his jeans. They fit kind of loose and a little bit baggy. They are not like Clint Black's jeans; they are not meant to be seen from the back. They fit, in fact, a little more like my own jeans do. In a way, I think, they are a lot more important than Garth's hat. Garth's hat actually makes him look sort of funny, in a loopy-voiced cute guy sort of way. His hat is part of his left-over-from-John-Travolta, city-gone-downscale image. It is part of his switcheroo game. It is part of the fun of javelin-tossing college boy Garth Brooks wearing cowboy boots and making over-the-break noises like po' boy Hank Williams, when it was sot-drunken Hank who wore welting-trimmed dress-up suits to prove his Alabama hick days were done. Hank's fans, however, believed what they were seeing, mainly because they believed what they heard. Garth—and Ricky and George and Clint—know perfectly well they're pretending. They've lip-synched their own voices too many times for VH-1.

Garth's jeans, however, are amazingly real. They are as real as the fact that he could stand to cut back on the fat grams. He calls himself "pudgy," which is something I know really well. He is not fat enough to be unfixable; neither is he Charlie Daniels-big. If Dwight Yoakam could be the country music Barbie, Garth could be its answer to Barney. He could dance around and have a little tummy overlap and still make kamillions of dollars making his happy little jolly-heartbreak sounds. He could be, in truth, the role model for katrillions of people like me, who could not only sound like him in the shower but look like him too.

I'm concerned, however, about that word "pudgy," the way he uses it when he gives interviews after receiving awards. I have a sense that it bothers him. It is not something he can cover up with a hairpiece or a black wide-brimmed hat. It is something he is trying hard to face. Late at night, when he is alone in a hotel room with a glass of room-service-order cocoa, I bet he looks out over the lights of a lonely city night and feels uneasy; I bet he gets the chubby cowboy blues.

I bet he goes to the window and looks down 115 stories into the traffic, which is full of taxicabs packed with rail-thin people on their way to nights full of rail-thin, non-sweaty love. I bet he thinks about the fact that, the next morning, none of those people will make a mad rush to the bathroom to put on a robe. I bet he wishes he had a burger and fries.

At that moment, if there were a song about love handles, I bet Garth Brooks could sing it. I bet it would hurt like Maria or Billie. I bet his voice would break with pain. I bet I would know just how he feels.

The Groaning Board

On Thanksgiving,
we chewed and kept quiet

 M y mother made it hard to like Thanksgiving. On Thanksgiving my mother would cook a turkey. She never got it right.

Sometime around the middle of October, every year, on a slanty-sunned Saturday morning, after a football game on the Friday night before, she would walk into my bedroom and say, "I need a piece of notebook paper. I've got to make a list."

I would look at the light lying low on the bedsheets, and I would realize we were already up to our necks in October. I would realize there was no way out. My mother was already Writing Things Down. It would do no good for other people to call and invite us to their houses. They would only end up eating at ours. My mother would say, "I've already got my list started. You can come eat over here." She would say, "No, I've got it all handled. You can just bring cranberry sauce in a can." They would only make her buy a bigger turkey. They would only make her candy more yams.

I would look at my band uniform lying in a purple-and-gold clump in the corner, and I would remember I didn't have any underwear on. I would pull the sheets up to my shoulders, and

I would lie. I would say, "I haven't got any notebook paper." I would say, "I'm feeling real sleepy right now."

I figured I needed the practice. Thanksgiving dinner was coming. In the next month, I would lie a lot more.

The lies would begin to mount up that same Saturday morning. I would walk into the kitchen, where my father's coffee cup was still in the sink. My mother would say, "Do you want coffee? I'll make some." I would say, "Yes," and the lies would begin. My mother would plug in the percolator and let whatever was inside it heat up. When the pot finished blurping, she would say, "I think your coffee's done." I would pour it in a cup and sit down to drink it. She would say, "I started it for Daddy. I hope it's not too strong by now." I would lie and say, "No. It's just fine."

Across the table, my mother would be writing on the back of an envelope. She would be using a blunt stubby pencil she had just sharpened with a serrated knife. She would say, "I'm having to make my list on the back of this envelope because nobody had any paper in this whole house."

I would pour cornflakes into a bowl and lie and say, "Gee, Mama, I'm sorry." She would say, "Now what do you think I should fix for Thanksgiving?" I would lie and say, "Whatever you cook will be fine." I would fear for the fate of my soul. She would say, "Your brother and your daddy said exactly the same thing." If I burned in hell, I would not burn alone.

My mother would say, "I think I'm tired of just old turkey." Then she would say, "But your daddy doesn't like to eat ham."

I would say, "On Thanksgiving, I think you have to have turkey." My mother would make a big heavy mark through the word "HAM?" on her envelope. She would write in "turkey" in the space right above it and right below "Ambrosia," which was the very first thing she had written in. She would underline "turkey" with a thin, shaky line. Then she would look uneasy and say, "Well, I'm *not* doing nutcups this year."

Nutcups were not my mother's problem. She could buy little foil cups and fill them up with cashews from the store. She could put them out on the table so that they would be there when everybody got there to sit down. She could grope her way blindly through a congealed-salad-on-a-bed-of-lettuce first course. She could fake it with a couple of mushroom-soup-casserole side dishes. She could chop up fruit and serve it with a slab of chocolate cake stirred up from a mix in a box. It was the turkey my mother did not understand.

Turkey was supposed to be meat, but she could not fry it. It did not make gravy, and it got cooked in a bag. It came with instructions about being roasted slowly with frequent basting of its own natural juices to preserve moisture and guarantee a succulent great golden bird. The turkey on the instruction-brochure cover was wearing a little pair of white-paper booties. It was surrounded by orange cups filled with sweet potatoes rich with brandy, topped with toasted-crispy marshmallows and slivers of brown-curly coconut and a sprinkling of grated orange zest.

My mother could not figure how such things could be caused to happen. Her mind did not have a setting for Succulent. She figured meat was either Raw or it was Done. She would save the instruction-brochure booklet and stuff it away in the back of a kitchen utensil drawer with all the pictures of orange-cupped turkeys from years before. This, she knew, was a picture of other people's turkeys. This was not how her turkey would be.

My mother would take her turkey out of the freezer on Monday and let it thaw on the sink for a couple of days. Then she would put it in the oven sometime on Wednesday and set it at something like 300 degrees. She would cook it until dawn the next day. Nobody ever caught anything. The turkey could not be carved at the table. It fell in big strings from the bone.

She brought it to the table on a big flowered china platter with no parsley around the edge. It was simply there when people got their nutcups. It was there when they prayed to give thanks.

My Aunt Birdie Mae said, "Sister, you're so good to have us."

My mother said, "We're glad you could be here. Families should be together on days like this." Then she would pass around the turkey, and everybody would chew and be quiet.

My Uncle Jesse said, "Sister, could I have a glass of water?"

My mother said, "I'm afraid the turkey's dried out. It's hard not to let it cook dry."

My Uncle Jesse said, "I bet it'll make a good sandwich."

My father said, "I bet I know what *I'll* be eating this week." Everybody laughed a hard little half-grunty laugh. "If I'm going to have me a leftover sandwich," my father said, "what I *really* want is a good slice of ham."

My mother went into the kitchen. When she came back she poured water in my Uncle Jesse's glass. For a while there was nothing but the sound of people chewing and the sound of ice cracking in glasses as the afternoon sun slipped in across the tablecloth.

After lunch—after the mix cake and the chopped-up-fruit ambrosia—people sat still at the table until they could go home.

My mother said, "Birdie Mae, why don't you take some of this turkey?"

My Aunt Birdie Mae said, "No, Sister, I've got my nutcup in my purse. It'll be my snack in the car on the way home."

That night my father ate his supper alone in the kitchen. He opened a can of sardines. He ate them with crackers while my mother stood beside the counter. She was using a little stubby blunt-nosed pencil. She was marking through words on a list.

Summer Romance

Somebody used a felt-tip;
it had to be love

THERE WERE three hand-addressed letters in my mailbox on a Saturday morning. They had not been mailed bulk rate, so I knew they could not be invitations. There were no flags anywhere on the envelopes, so I knew they had nothing to do with a congressional campaign. Because they were addressed by hand, I knew they were not asking me to write a check to prevent the abuse of small animals. Because they did not say, "Second Notice," I knew they had not come from anybody who wanted me to pay them for a Patsy Cline CD.

Because they were addressed by hand—and even though I was not in love when I went to my mailbox at eleven o'clock on this particular Saturday morning—I figured I had probably received at least one love letter. It did not matter that none of the handwriting suggested anybody I knew. These were letters written by people without time to get to a typewriter; clearly, they included words it would not be appropriate for a secretary to hear.

Any one of these letters, I knew, could be the pain wracked confession of a heart grown weary after beating too hard for too long against the walls of one frail human chest. Somewhere in these letters, there would have to be a confession of undying devotion. Anything else could have been said over the phone.

When I read these letters, I knew, I would need to be gentle. When I opened them, I did not want to be alone. I wanted other people to be watching. I went into the kitchen and popped the ring-top on a Fresca. I took my three letters and went down to the pool.

At the pool, even before I could take off my T-shirt, my friend Byron said, "My God, you got hand-addressed mail!"

I said, "Byron, in this world, there are still a few people who feel the need to write things. I figure there's a good chance that one of these letters may be very painful. One of them may even be a letter about love." I said, "Before I start reading them, I may need to borrow some block."

Byron tossed me his block tube and said, "I think hand-written letters are always dramatic." He said, "If you don't mind, when you open the envelopes, I'll just lie here on the chaise longue and watch." I said that Byron should not be surprised if the content of these letters was deeply personal and fraught with emotion. Byron said, "Do you think it would be all right if Angie came over and watched too?"

Angie was wearing a two-piece and drinking Evian out of a sports bottle. She sat down on the edge of Byron's chaise longue and picked up one of my letters. She said, "Wow, what kind of software package do you think these people use?"

I said, "Angie, what you are seeing here are hand-addressed letters. They were written by a person holding a pen."

Angie said, "Wow, that is absolutely amazing. I bet that took somebody a lot of time. How many people do you figure they had on their list?"

I said, "Angie, these are what are known as *personal* letters. Each of them includes a unique and individual message. People write this sort of letter when they want to say something important, something you may want to savor many years later when you have grown bitter with the world and have forgotten you have ever been loved. Letters such as these are often quite intimate. The people who write them struggle and agonize over the choice of each grueling word."

Angie said, "I guess that means they couldn't just leave a message on your machine."

Byron said, "Think about it, Angie. In old movies, people get letters like this all the time."

Angie said, "I never saw that kind of thing in a Jane Fonda movie."

Byron said, "I mean older movies than that — I mean movies with Joseph Cotten and Jennifer Jones and Bette Davis and Joan Fontaine. In Bette Davis movies everybody has really nice penmanship, and they write these wonderful letters that either get mailed to the wrong person or Joan Fontaine's husband finds them under the lavender sachet in her handkerchief drawer. If people didn't know how to write letters, nothing would ever go wrong in a black-and-white movie. If people didn't write letters, there would never be any plots in black-and-white movies at all."

Angie said, "I never write letters, and I never have any of those problems."

Byron said, "That, Angie, is because there is no *suspense* in your existence. It is very difficult to have suspense on a cordless phone."

Angie said she was afraid she was getting burned on her shoulders. She said, if I didn't read my letters now, she would have to go in. But, she said, she really wanted to be there when my letters were opened. Angie said she had never heard of anybody being in love and being willing to write it down.

Using my pool key for a letter opener, I opened each of my envelopes carefully. I made sure they did not get stained with lotion. I made sure they did not get struck too suddenly by the sun. Byron watched me silently through the lenses of his Ray-Bans. Angie leaned forward from the edge of the chaise longue.

Two of the letters were from insurance agents congratulating me on my forty-second birthday. The third letter was from a Baptist church inviting me to participate in its singles group, which met every Friday in a restaurant with a salad bar.

I did not read the letters aloud to Byron and Angie. Instead, I slipped each of the letters back into its envelope. I weighted each of the letters down under my Fresca can.

Angie said, "OK. So which one was the love letter?"

Byron said, "My God, Angie, don't you know when you're witnessing something really personal?"

Angie said, "I'm getting out of here. I've got a beeper to check."

She wrapped her pool towel around her and asked me if I was planning to recycle my envelopes. She reminded me that each of my envelopes had, probably, at some time been a tree.

As Angie walked around the edge of the pool, gathering up her magazines, I told her I figured my envelopes were my own problem. I said I would probably treat them and their letters in pretty much the same way. While her shadow moved across the pool's surface, I picked up my letters and slipped them under my towel. Watching my letters through the green-black lenses of his sunglasses, Byron whispered, "We live in a world where there is no more poetry." I rolled over on top of my letters. "Some things," I whispered to Byron, "lose all their beauty when they are said aloud."

High and Dry

Did Fred Astaire ever
really order dinner?

 A MAN WHO drinks martinis would rather die than wear brown shoes in public. He is the man who is always seen in the company of women in Chanel. He never rents his evening clothes. He has never been elected to public office.

He never drinks before six. And—except for moments of great world-weariness or late nights filled with memories of songs written before 1942—he never, never drinks alone.

For him, the martini is not an affectation. He does not think it makes him look like Adolphe Menjou. His date does not want to look like Myrna Loy. Neither of them wants to be mistaken for anyone who has ever met Donald Trump.

They expect their martinis, and they expect them now—very cold, very dry, up, with an olive. They equate the standard formula—four-parts gin, one part vermouth—with Singapore Slings and pink rum drinks mixed in a blender. The merest mention of the word "vermouth" will do quite-nicely-thank-you. Anything more is a recipe for punch.

They assume they need not mention "Shaken-Not-Stirred." They do not speak of "bruising the gin."

At table, their conversation never turns to politics or the children's grades in school. Instead, they plan trips to the South of France and try to remember the names of small cafes in the Piazza San Marco.

They lift their glasses. The long, slow, stinging edge of the martini's blade slides in. The olive, still salty and angry but soaked with the scent of flowers, they save for last. Wherever they are, it is El Morocco. Whatever the year, it is 1932. The miracle of the One True Cocktail has kicked in.

Its wonders, however, are not merely there for the ordering. They are a privilege to be earned. The martini calls unto itself a secret society, consisting entirely of persons who have never learned the words to anything by John Denver or read an interview with Vanna White. Persons who do not know anyone with a tattoo.

I have no proof of it, but I'll bet that the first time I ever saw a martini, it was being drunk by Fred Astaire. (It couldn't have been Bogart, who always ordered whiskey; it was always served by people with tattoos.) Invariably, Fred was out of a job. Still, he was making do with a hotel suite in one of London's posher neighborhoods. The walls, of course, were white with platinum-chromium trim, and Ginger Rogers lived downstairs, a cocked derringer of a woman in bias-cut charmeuse.

Despite Fred's reduced circumstances, there was always a valet. And there were always martinis. They were never asked for; they simply appeared, gliding in on a silver tray.

"Your cocktail, Sir," the valet would announce with an extravagant little lisp that made it difficult for him to pronounce his R's.

"Thank you, Huggleby," Fred would say. He would take the glass from the tray and lift it to the light so that it sparkled in the silver soundstage air. Then he would dance. Downstairs, Ginger would call the management; romance was inescapable.

Barely touched by the curve of Fred's six-inch fingers, the martini was a marquis diamond, facet-cut, quivering icily on its crystal stem. Fred himself was a lonely sliver of black worsted wool with sleek satin trim. It was a meeting of icons.

The martini's origins are vague at best. Clearly, its name suggests northern Italy, but its heritage is inarguably British. Flaunting a rather unlikely—and potentially lethal—mix of fermented and distilled liquors, it may well have been developed in a moment of desperation, perhaps in a field hospital somewhere behind the lines during the Boer War. (In similarly trying times, a decade or so later, the British would, lest we forget, take to mixing champagne and gin in shell casings in the trenches at Ypres and Verdun.)

After the Great War, however, the martini hit the streets of New York. And it was home. Not even Prohibition could slow its gradual takeover of café society. By the Thirties, the martini had developed its own mythology. Its mystic rituals demanded shakers, stirrers, strainers, and glasses—the sleek, cool-edged tools of Art Deco bachelordom. Its preparation had been rarefied into a holy rite. Then by 1955, with the advent of TV dinners, pedal pushers, and Elvis, the martini was doomed. Beer came in cans. Easiness was all.

But still, the ideal persisted. In Des Moines and Grand Rapids, in Tampa and Toledo, wherever liquor was served by women in white middy blouses with red handkerchief corsages pinned to their bosoms, a martini glass, sketched in white neon, with a green neon olive stuck on a blue neon toothpick, blinked and sputtered in the fume-filled air. Women in fishnet hose and men with tattoos popped open cool ones and served beer nuts in ceramic dishes shaped like the state of Wisconsin.

And still the martini glowed on. Even now, though, when the day has been fiercely ruthless—or better still, when the night promises to grow especially silken and Chanel bracelets rattle on a banquette nearby—its moment arrives again. On such evenings, the first taste of the gin, brittle and cold, stings and stabs at the tongue. The whiff of vermouth etherizes the entire undertaking. Each sip becomes seduction and solace, both at once. Every man begins to move like Fred Astaire in a white-furnished suite at Claridge's. Ere long, conversation turns to the south of France.

On such evenings, we learn that this is a cocktail. On such evenings, everything else is just hooch.

Some Place Cool

I'd trade every Stuckey's on the highway for one more Nehi-drinking bear

MY MOTHER did not like the beach. She had never been there, and she did not want to go. She knew what it would be like: It would be hot, and there would be people in damp swimsuits still scratchy with bits of leftover day-before sand. There would be fretful children with water in their ears, and somebody would step on something and need a shot.

The year I was five, she gave fair warning sometime after supper on a slow June evening when the sun was taking a long, mild time to set. She made her position known before anyone had even breathed the word "Vacation."

"If we're going anywhere," she decreed, standing at the sink while the low, mild sun stained the front of her housedress orange, "I want to go some place cool.

"If we go to Florida," she said, wiping the soapsuds from her hands and slipping her wedding ring back over her dishwater-crinkly knuckles, "I'll just get my head wet and it'll never get dry." My mother did not own a swimsuit. She had never been wet all over in her life.

For the sake of her hair, we headed up and out of Alabama,

to a place my mother said would be green and cold. She had packed our winter jackets.

Before we had reached Birmingham, she started breathing in big deep breaths of the hot Alabama air that blistered the sides of the car. She held her hand out in the stinging-hot wind, and she sang. The wind slapped against her flat-open palm and she sang, "In the Blue Ridge Mountains of Virginia, in the Trail of the Lonesome Pine." She would sing those words again and again. They were the only words she knew.

The car was a Junebug-green Buick. It was bigger than the room where my brother and I slept. It was big enough that we could play in the floorboard, rolling each other over and over the hump and laughing until my father had to stop the car before we had even reached Tuscumbia. He took us out and talked to us on the side of the road.

Back in the car, my mother told him, "It was not The Baby's fault." She was not smiling. Her words formed a hard little line. "This is going to be a long trip, Margaret," my father said. Then he turned the key so hard that the engine made a rackety racheting noise. My mother looked straight ahead at the highway. She looked hard at the road flying past. She held her hand out to hit the wind.

Somewhere outside of Chattanooga it began to get cool. My mother said, "Roll the windows down, Daddy, so the boys can get the breeze." He pushed a switch on the dashboard, and the windows buzzed down in the back. The air from the mountains rushed in and made the car cool. My brother held his head out the window and the wind blew his hair back in a stiff little sheet. I climbed up on the seat so the wind could blow my hair back too.

"One time a little boy stuck his head out the window of a Buick," my father said without looking back, even into the mirror. "His daddy drove too close to a lightpole and it popped that little boy's head off before they even knew it was gone. It went Pop, and it was over like that."

"Pull your head in, Baby," my mother said. "And Bubba, you can pull your head in too."

"But there's not any lightpoles on this side," said my brother, his words flying back past him in the wind.

"Pull your head in," said my father, "or the window goes up. Pull your head in and start counting cows. You can make it a contest."

"The Baby can't count," said my mother.

"Then he can watch for license plates," said my father.

"He can't read," said my mother. "He can't watch for license plates if he can't read."

"I forgot," said my father.

"He doesn't start first grade until this year," my mother said.

"I forgot," said my father.

"I have to go to the bathroom," said my brother.

I said, "I have to go to the bathroom too."

"You can't go to the bathroom now," said my father. "There's no place to stop. It'll be Gatlinburg before you can go."

My brother said, "I have to go to the bathroom now. I saw a sign for a place with a bear. I want to go there."

I said, "I want to got to the bathroom." I said, "I want to go to the bathroom with the bear."

The bear lived in a cage behind a gas station. It sat on its hind legs and drank chocolate Nehis for a living. In the picture out front, the bear's coat was black and shiny with highlights of near-black glistening blue. Out back the bear was brown for the most part with big flat patches of unshiny gray.

"That's a pretty old bear," said my father.

My brother said, "He hasn't got any teeth."

"It's the Nehis," said the guy who ran the station. "In a day he gets two dozen. It's educational for the kids. People come see this bear from six states."

My mother said, "I need the keys. I'm going back to the car. I need to let the windows down."

That night we stopped in a motel before Asheville. The motel was a whole little town of tiny white houses — each one round-cornered, each one covered in white cement. In our house my mother was making sandwiches with bread she had brought from Alabama and sliced meat she had bought that afternoon at the store. In the bathroom my father was brushing his teeth.

"I want to go to the swimming pool," said my brother.

I said, "I want to go to the swimming pool too."

"You can't go to the pool now," said my mother. "I'm making sandwiches for supper."

"Let them go," said my father, through the half-cocked bathroom door.

"Go on," said my mother. "But don't get wet. You can't go in. You've had mumps."

My brother and I stood by the fence, looking in at the pool. There were still wasps coming down to the water to drink, but they were too cool and sleepy to sting. The white of the cabins was turning pale gray.

"I'm hungry," said my brother. Then I turned to see him, and he was gone.

"We're in 5-A," he called from the darkness. "Don't go in the pool. You'll give people mumps." From the darkness I heard a door slam.

I ran after him into the twilight, along the flat white row of little just-alike houses marked with black wrought-iron numbers I was scheduled to learn the next year. Above each doorway, an egg-yellow light bulb had been switched on. In each plate-glass sliding window, the Venetian blinds were pulled shut so that people could not look in.

I was afraid that if I could see around the edge into any window, I would not see my parents. I was afraid that if I saw them I would not know who they were. I was afraid I would knock on the wrong window and make somebody mad.

The air around me on the sidewalk was cold. I wanted to go to the bathroom very bad.

Behind me, in a minute there was my brother. "Mama says to
get you for supper," he said. I turned to see him, looking orangy
in the bug light, and my father in the doorway, standing in his
sock feet. From the cabin my mother was singing "In the Trail
of the Lonesome Pine." I went to the door and watched.

She was setting out sandwiches, made with bread she had
brought from Alabama in a bag. She had opened the plate-glass
window so that the air from the mountains poured in. The
breeze made the fringe on the bedspread move. The air made
the room very cool.